A GUT HEALTH JOURNEY

A GUIDE TO LIVING IN HARMONY
WITH YOUR BODY

EMMA CANNINGS

To everyone who has loved and supported me along the way.
You know who you are. Thank you. xx

Contents

My Story	1
Why This Book Exists	10
Why THERA Nordic Exists	15
Why You're (Maybe) Reading This Book	20
The Six Core Pillars of Health	23
How Your Gut Works	35
Common Gut Health Myths	42
Gut Health & Your Skin	50
Hormones & Gut Health	58
Travel & Gut Health	67
The Critical Role of Fibre	73
Gut Health Advice for Parents	81
Mental Health & Gut Health: The Hidden Connection	91
The Future of Gut Health	97

Client Stories	108
Closing Chapter: Your Gut Healing Journey Starts Here	129
Appendix I: References & Further Reading	134
Appendix II: Recipes	141
Appendix III: Using THERA Nordic Products	163

My Story

Hi, I'm Emma. I wanted to start this book by sharing my own story about my personal gut health journey. I hope it will provide some context as to why I'm writing this book and perhaps even some inspiration for others who might be struggling with their own gut health.

I was born in 1981 in Johannesburg, South Africa, and I'm the eldest of three children. I spent my early years in Johannesburg before leaving at the age of 12. My time in South Africa was a mix of happiness, illness, and feeling lost.

I attended a prestigious all-girls private school, but it quickly became clear that I didn't fit in. My brain didn't work like the other girls', and I felt completely out of my depth—an outsider. I struggled with severe dyslexia, making every task a challenge. It was frustrating and embarrassing, like being a fish out of water.

I was prescribed Ritalin, a drug typically used for ADHD, even though I wasn't showing signs of it at the time. The medication suppressed my appetite, and I became seriously thin and unwell. I despised school so much that I often pretended to be sick to avoid going. Between my real illness from malnutrition and my fake illnesses, I spent a lot of time at doctors' appointments. Back in the '80s, antibiotics were the go-to solution for almost everything, so I was frequently given them—whether I needed them or not. Looking back, I believe this constant exposure to antibiotics was the root cause of my gut health issues. While antibiotics are lifesaving when necessary, overuse can wreak havoc on the gut microbiome.

At 12, my life took a major turn when we moved to the UK. Adjusting was tough. The school I attended had little to no focus on education or grades, and I quickly became a rebel. Instead of learning, my focus shifted to how much trouble I could get into. I was the black sheep of the family and a bit of a nightmare. I left school with pretty much nothing to show for it.

Despite that, I threw myself into work, taking on any job I could find. Luckily, I had the best friend in the world by my side, and together, we worked long days, nights, and weekends, navigating life in our own way.

Striving to be financially independent was always important for me. However, I knew I did not want to spend my life working all hours, 7 days a week, day or night for minimum wage. I had to do something more for myself. The only path that remotely interested me with the qualifications I had, and offered the freedom to travel the world, was an NVQ in Beauty Therapy. So, I enrolled in a course while still juggling all my other jobs.

Studying became my saviour. I was never interested in painting nails or applying makeup. What truly fascinated me was the human body. Anatomy and physiology got me! We studied the human body and the skin in depth. To my amazement, I discovered that I loved learning! I just needed to be passionate about the subject. And this, I loved.

My learning extended far beyond the classroom. I devoured books, clinical studies, online courses, and any science I could get my hands on. This became my passion. After completing college, I continued working in the field, specialising in skin health, the body, and how diet and lifestyle influence both. I worked in clinics before eventually setting up my own practice.

My career took me to Spain, where I treated the rich and famous before opening my own salon and hiring a team to work alongside me. Over time, my interests and studies expanded to nutrition and personal training, leading me to establish a solo clinic where I offered personalised fitness and personal nutrition plans. Watching my clients grow stronger, healthier, and more confident was incredibly rewarding.

At age 25, while running my salon, I became a mother—something I had always dreamed of. From a young age, I had imagined the baby I would love and care for all my life. In February 2006, my first perfect, healthy little girl was born, and 18 months later, my second. I felt completely whole. I had been gifted with two incredible daughters, and it became my mission to give them the best start in life.

Anyone who knows me can attest to how much I prioritised their diet and health. My girls would happily snack on an entire steamed broccoli. I was always frustrated with the "kids' menu" and felt that they were never a great help for parents or kids. Why should adults get a well-thought-out, balanced menu while children are left with chicken nuggets and pizza? I wanted to make sure that my children were exposed to real, nourishing food vegetables, fruits, and hearty meals. But I appreciate that it's so hard (and seems to be getting harder!) for parents with modern lifestyles.

I know first-hand that getting kids to eat well isn't always easy—it takes effort, patience, and consistency. But I promise, the hard work pays off. To this day, my daughters naturally gravitate toward healthier choices and rarely eat processed or junk foods.

In my quest to study longevity and health, I unknowingly took myself down an unhealthy rabbit hole. I've always been passionate about optimising well-being, but I lost sight of one crucial thing—balance. The combination of my growing obsession and the isolation of lockdown during covid tipped the scales for me.

I became completely consumed by "biohacking". If there was a new health-enhancing tool on the market, I had to have it. I was taking endless supplements, meticulously timing my meals, and obsessing over every detail—from ensuring my water was filtered and re-mineralised, to stressing over anything remotely "off track" in my diet. My morning and evening routines became so rigid and unsustainable that they started to take over my life. I was pushing people away because they disrupted my strict discipline.

Looking back, I now recognise this pattern in others, and it makes me sad. It's a lonely place to be. The irony is that human connection and reducing stress are far more important for longevity than any rigid, regimented health routine. I had turned myself into my own lab rat, sacrificing happiness in the pursuit of perfection.

It was during one of my "biohacking" health retreats in Estonia that I met Joni. We quickly became close friends, bonding over our shared passion for health and science. His story intrigued me—he was the founder of the largest supplement company in Scandinavia and had developed hundreds of formulations. He had since sold his former company but held onto one product that he was particularly proud of: REZCUE.

REZCUE was originally created by Joni to help a loved one who was struggling with severe gut health issues. The formula was designed to heal stomach ulcers, but he quickly realised its benefits extended far beyond that—it was improving overall digestive health. Soon, customers were sharing life-changing stories. People were experiencing relief from heartburn, indigestion, and ulcers, and even more severe conditions like Crohn's disease and colitis were showing incredible improvement.

Despite its remarkable effects, REZCUE was only selling in Finland, with a small presence in the US and UK through Amazon. It was just *ticking over*, but the world needed to know about it. This wasn't just another supplement—it was something truly special.

One day, Joni asked me if I'd be interested in bringing REZCUE to the UK and starting a company based here. Without hesitation, I knew this was the right path. There wasn't a doubt in my mind.

I set up the company in the UK, updated the brand, and gradually wound down my own clinic. Joni and I worked together to develop the brand, ensuring that everything we created aligned with our core values. From the beginning, we were committed to building a 100% clean, honest, and transparent company—one that upheld the highest standards possible.

Over time, we expanded our collection of products, but we always stuck to one key principle: we follow science, not trends. Of course, science evolves, and we remain open-minded, always staying informed about new emerging research.

It was only at this point—after years of obsessively trying to optimise my health—that I was finally able to fix my own gut issues. Despite my extreme biohacking routines, my gut problems had never truly disappeared. The damage from years of childhood antibiotics still had a hold on me.

I started with REZCUE, using it to heal, soothe, and protect my digestive tract. While it offered some relief, I was still struggling—every time I ate, I experienced gas and bloating. I became convinced that I was intolerant to most foods. Turns out, I wasn't! The real issue? I was severely lacking stomach acid.

For me, our Triple HCL product (a betaine HCL supplement to naturally boost your stomach acid levels if they are low) was life changing. And I don't say that lightly—it literally transformed my health. Anyone who knows me knows this because I shout it from the rooftops! When you've suffered from gut issues for so long, finally feeling better is the best feeling in the world.

I can genuinely say that I'm my own biggest advocate for our products, and that feels amazing. I cycle through them all and take Daily Healthy Fibre every day. Our products have been a game-changer for me, and I love sharing that with others.

I now take fewer supplements than I have in years, knowing that my fibre-rich diet provides me with far more nutrients—now that my body can properly digest food.

I'm incredibly passionate about what I do, and nothing is more rewarding than knowing we've helped someone. We frequently hear life-changing success stories, and it fuels my mission even more. I truly believe that better gut health leads to a more peaceful, balanced life, and I want that for the world.

I hope you enjoy my book and that it brings you valuable insights on your own journey to better health.

Why This Book Exists

If you're reading this book the chances are that you, or someone you care about, are struggling with gut issues. Whether it's bloating, constipation, diarrhoea, acid reflux, heartburn, indigestion, SIBO, or Candida, living with digestive problems can take over your life. It affects how you eat, how you feel, and how you show up in the world.

I wrote this book because I wanted to try and help make sense of the confusing world of gut health. There's so much information out there—some good, some misleading—and it can leave people feeling lost, overwhelmed, and hopeless.

I want to emphasise that I'm not a doctor. So why should you listen to any of my advice?! Social media in particular is full of "good advice" on diets and supplements. And whilst there are some amazing people in the biohacking community, it's also a space that is full of pseudoscience and claims that a particular approach to gut health is "life-changing" simply because it happened to change that individual's life. I think partially this book is a reaction to my frustration of seeing so much bad advice online. Our bodies are all unique, and what works for one person will not always have the same effect on another. Some people will swear that the carnivore diet changed their lives whilst others will make the same claim about becoming a vegan. And the same is true of the claims that people make about supplements that they try. Many people are taking so many supplements that it's almost impossible to scientifically claim what is actually creating any benefits that they may feel. As I've said already, Triple HCL was particularly life-changing for me, but that doesn't mean that it will help everyone since it really depends on the underlying condition that you have.

All I can claim is that I've spent years consuming as many books and scientific papers as possible. Working with Joni and formulating supplements has given me a deeper knowledge, and I also credit Joni for helping me take a more scientific approach to my health. So, whilst I'm sure there are parts of this book that I will iterate on and improve over time, I hope I can provide a balanced view based on the latest science in the world of gut health, and not just another "fad" book based on an unscientific theory or the fact that something happened to work for me! At the end of the book, I've referenced a few of the key books and scientific papers that have been particularly inspirational for me, and I can highly recommend them as further reading for anyone who would like to delve further into this subject.

Through real-life stories, practical tips, recipes, and guidance, my hope is that this book will become a companion on your healing journey—something that makes you feel less alone, and more empowered to take the right steps for *you*.

At THERA Nordic, we're known for creating targeted supplements for gut health—but at our core, we are about so much more than just supplements. We believe in real healing, which means understanding the root cause of digestive issues, nurturing the body, and supporting it in a way that goes beyond relying on products long-term.

Our vision is to help you live a more peaceful life through improved gut health. We want to help you to rebuild a healthy gut so you can live a full life—where food is joyful again, and you aren't tied to endless pills and powders in order to function. Supplements can be powerful tools when used wisely, but they are only part of the bigger picture.

Whether you are just starting out on your gut healing journey, or you've been battling these issues for years, this book is for you.

From Joni and me, we want you to know that you deserve to feel good in your body again—and we're here to help you get there.

💡 Quick Tip: Eat in a Relaxed State

Slow down before meals. Sit down, take a few deep breaths, and focus on your food.

Avoid eating on the go, when stressed, or distracted digestion works best when you're calm

Why THERA Nordic Exists

Our roots, vision and mission

Our roots are grounded in personal healing and scientific integrity. What started as a conversation between two health enthusiasts, myself and my co-founder Joni, evolved into a mission-driven company.

We have always been aligned in our vision; to help people live a more peaceful life through improved gut health. We wanted to create a transparent, honest, and uncompromising brand that helps people regain control of their health, starting from the gut outward.

Our mission is simple; to consciously develop our products using ingredients that we would be happy to give to a loved family member. We want to ensure that we:

- Empower people to heal naturally
- Offer products that are backed by science, not trends
- Support gut health as the foundation for overall well-being

The science behind our approach

At THERA Nordic, science comes first. Every product we create is rooted in scientific evidence, and real-world results. We don't follow trends; we follow data. We also remain open to evolving science, always ready to adapt as new research emerges.

Our formulas focus on addressing the root cause of issues, not just masking symptoms. Whether it's restoring the gut lining, balancing the microbiome, or supporting digestion, we aim to create effective, targeted solutions that are clean, safe, and backed by research.

Natural healing and the role of supplementation

The body has an incredible ability to heal itself if given the right support. Nutrition and lifestyle will always be the foundation of health, but sometimes we need additional support to bridge the gaps created by modern living, chronic stress, and environmental factors.

That's where targeted supplementation comes in—to restore balance, rebuild strength, and support the healing process. Our supplements are carefully formulated to work *with* the body, using natural, effective, and bioavailable ingredients that enhance what your body is already capable of doing.

The team behind THERA Nordic

Joni, our co-founder, brings decades of experience in supplement formulation and was the creator of REZCUE, our flagship product. His commitment to quality and integrity set the foundation for everything we do.

I was driven by personal healing and a relentless pursuit of knowledge, I bring my experience in skin health, nutrition, and lifestyle medicine to ensure we always think holistically about health.

Together, we are a team that cares deeply about helping people—not just selling products. We listen, we learn, and we evolve—because at the heart of THERA Nordic is a genuine desire to make a difference.

Our journey in health and wellness

Our journey has been anything but linear. Like many of you, we've experienced the frustration of feeling unwell, trying everything, and the long search for answers. We've walked the path of trial and error, spent years studying, and learned from both science and real-life experience.

THERA Nordic is the result of that journey—a brand built on resilience, passion, and a belief that healing is possible. Today, we continue to learn and grow, always focused on our vision to help others live more peaceful, healthier, happier lives through improved gut health.

💡 Quick Tip: Support Stomach Acid Levels

Consider natural ways to support stomach acid, like **apple cider vinegar (1 tsp in water before meals) or lemon water** — unless these don't suit you or you've been advised otherwise by your doctor.

Why You're (Maybe) Reading This Book

If you've picked up this book, there's a good chance you're searching for answers, and I want you to know that you are *not* alone.

If you can relate to any of the following, you are in the same boat as about 90% of the people I speak to daily:

- You're focused on fixing symptoms instead of addressing the root cause—whether that's avoiding entire food groups because of intolerances, relying on antacids or PPIs for heartburn, or using laxatives to "get things moving."
- You often feel bloated, especially after eating, and have no idea why.
- You're struggling with heartburn, indigestion, constipation—or sometimes all of the above.
- You're ignoring stress and poor sleep, not realising just how much they impact your gut health.
- You've tried endless cleanses, detoxes, and extreme diets, hoping they'd fix everything—only to end up right back where you started.
- You hope supplements can fix your issues, without realising that no pill can undo a poor diet and lifestyle (a hard truth, I know!).
- You're taking probiotics because you've been told they're good for you—without fully understanding

what they do, if you even need them, or how they work in your body.

If *any* of this sounds familiar, you're in the right place. My goal with this book is to help you understand what's really going on in your gut, why you're struggling, and how to finally take steps that actually make a difference—without falling into another extreme or fad. Let's get started!

💡 Quick Tip: Move Your Body Daily

Gentle movement like walking, yoga, stretching, or swimming **stimulates digestion** and helps prevent sluggish bowels.

Aim for **at least 20–30 minutes a day**, even if it's just a walk after meals.

The Six Core Pillars of Health

Like many people, myself included, the chances are you've tried "fixing" your gut through elimination diets, endless supplements, or maybe even extreme cleanses — and yet, you perhaps still feel stuck.

The truth is, gut health isn't built on one magic bullet, but on a foundation of daily habits and balanced living. Lasting gut health is connected strongly to your overall health, and I focus on six key pillars. If you can address these, everything else starts to fall into place. The six key pillars are:

- Diet
- Movement
- Sleep
- Stress management
- Community
- Targeted supplements

I know it can be overwhelming (and how many times are we told to eat better, exercise more, improve our sleep and reduce our stress levels!). But if you can make small changes to each one, over time they make a huge difference. And if you are spending money on supplements, it's critical that you try and work on the areas that might be the cause of the underlying issues.

Let's dive into each of them.

1. Diet: The Foundation of Gut Health

When it comes to healing and supporting your gut, what you eat is the most powerful tool you have. If you put water in the fuel tank of your car you will create all sorts of problems! The same is true of your body. The foods you choose shape your microbiome, influence digestion, and either support or sabotage your health.

But with so much conflicting advice, it's easy to get overwhelmed or trapped in unhealthy extremes. Scientific studies point to the importance of a balanced, bio-individual approach — no one-size-fits-all solutions, just real food that supports real healing.

Focus on Whole, Nutrient-Dense Foods

Your gut thrives on real, minimally processed foods that nourish beneficial bacteria and support digestive health. Try and make sure you can tick as many of these boxes as possible with your diet:

- Try to consume enough animal or plant-based proteins — grass-fed meat, wild-caught fish, organic eggs, legumes (if tolerated), tofu.

- Healthy fats are so important! — extra virgin olive oil, avocado, nuts, seeds, omega-3s from fish
- Colourful fruits and vegetables are packed with fibre, antioxidants, and polyphenols
- Fermented foods — sauerkraut, kefir, kimchi, yogurt, miso (if tolerated)

Life is hard and you can't be good all the time (in fact that would not be much fun!). I try and work on an 80 / 20 rule by eating well most of the time and not worrying about the odd treats.

Avoid Common Gut Disruptors

Some foods actively damage the gut lining or promote inflammation, including:

- Highly processed foods (refined sugars, artificial additives, preservatives)
- Excess refined grains (white flour, packaged snacks)
- Artificial sweeteners (can disrupt microbiome balance and cause bloating)

It is almost impossible to cut these out completely these days. Just be aware of the unseen damage that these can do to your gut.

One way to start is to avoid having these types of foods at home, even if you just start by stopping the habit of picking up snacks from the supermarket. If you can eat cleaner at home, and relax when you are out socialising, that's still a great step!

Eat in a Way That Supports Digestion

It's not just what you eat — but *how* you eat that impacts digestion:

- Chew thoroughly — digestion starts in the mouth; give your body a head start.
- Avoid eating on-the-go — stress shuts down digestion. Sit, relax, and savor.
- Time meals wisely — consider spacing meals or gentle intermittent fasting to give your digestive system a break (if appropriate for you).

Personalise Your Diet

Remember: your gut is unique. Some people thrive on high-fibre, plant-based diets; others need lower FODMAP* or more animal based approaches. Listen to your body and choose foods that:

- Make you feel energised and satisfied.
- Support regular bowel movements.

- Don't leave you bloated, inflamed, or foggy.

FODMAP stands for fermentable oligosaccharides, disaccharides, monosaccharides, and polyols, which are short-chain carbohydrates that some people with digestive issues find difficult to digest, potentially leading to symptoms like bloating, gas, and diarrhea. You can find lists of FODMAP foods with a quick search on the Internet as well as plans to show you how to identify the foods that are causing you the most issues.

Key takeaway: Skip the fads. But also avoid getting sucked into a particular diet because someone else was raving about how amazing it has been for them. As I pointed out earlier, this is a common issue with social media today! It might not work for you. Prioritise real, whole foods that work for *your* body — and build habits you can maintain long-term.

2. Movement: The Role of Activity in Digestion and Health

Movement is about so much more than just "fitness". As an ex-personal trainer, my fitness routine is important for me. But this book is not a fitness book, and this section is not about convincing you to get to the gym every day!

Regular movement stimulates digestion, promotes circulation, and helps manage stress — all essential for gut health.

Simple daily movement like walking after meals, stretching, or gentle yoga can help food move through the digestive tract, reduce bloating, and even improve gut motility.

You don't need to overtrain (in fact this can lead to leaky gut and other issues!) — just move your body regularly and find activities that bring you joy. One of the main focusses of my daily routine is to try and go for a short walk around the block after lunch or dinner to minimise blood glucose spikes and support digestion.

3. Sleep, Rest & Digest: Why Recovery Is Key

Rest and recovery are often overlooked, but they are vital for gut repair and overall health. Poor sleep increases gut permeability ("leaky gut"), raises stress hormones, and affects digestion.

Prioritising seven to nine hours of good quality sleep and allowing your body to rest and repair is as crucial as diet. Remember, your body heals when you're at rest. When your body is tired and stressed your digestive system will struggle to do its job effectively.

Intermittent fasting effects people in different ways (again, it's not a one-size fits all solution). Personally, I try to avoid eating after about 6pm. I keep my circadian rhythm in sync by being fairly strict with my bedtime where I can. For me, it's usually 9.30/10pm to 6am (although my stress levels will determine how much of that I'm actually asleep for!). By the time I'm eating breakfast at 7am I've given my gut at least 13 hours to recover. That works really well for me so perhaps give it a try and experiment with the timings to see how it affects your body.

When I do need to go out and eat later, that's when I'll always use a supplement to help me (for me, you might not be surprised to hear, it's Triple HCL, but more on that later!).

4. Stress Management: The Gut-Brain Connection

Your gut and brain are deeply connected — stress and anxiety can directly harm digestion, cause inflammation, and disrupt the microbiome.

Chronic stress is one of the biggest obstacles to gut healing. Incorporating daily stress-reduction practices like deep breathing, meditation, nature walks, or even simple "unplugged" time can reset your nervous system and help the gut function optimally.

If you're doing "all the right things" with food and supplements but ignoring stress, you're missing a major piece of the puzzle. I do appreciate that this is much easier said than done with modern lifestyles. Recently I've really changed the types of people that I follow on social media (I am not a huge fan, but it is important for the business!). Just a few small changes over time can have a big impact. Later in this book there is a chapter on the connection between gut health and mental health, so we'll drill into this in a little more detail.

5. Connections & Community: The Impact of Relationships on Health

Humans are wired for connection. Although we live in an increasingly connected world, in many ways that can place a barrier that damages the real human connections that we evolved to need.

Loneliness and isolation are forms of chronic stress that negatively affect the gut microbiome and immune system. There have been a lot of scientific studies showing that a strong community leads to reductions in stress and longer, healthier lifespans

Building and maintaining meaningful relationships supports emotional well-being, reduces stress, and promotes physical health. Even simple, positive interactions can help regulate the nervous system and improve digestion.

The healing power of community and connection is starting to gain real scientific backing — we were never meant to do this alone. Most of us have had feelings of loneliness in our lives. Sometimes it just takes that extra bit of effort to pick up the phone to a friend instead of sending a message. Or finding someone to go for a walk with and tick off two pillars of health at the same time!

6. Support Through Supplements: Using Them Wisely, Not as a Crutch

I have always believed that supplements should support your body, not replace a healthy diet and lifestyle.

At THERA Nordic, we focus on targeted, science-backed formulations designed to address specific needs — like rebuilding the gut lining, supporting digestion, and restoring the balance of your gut microbiome.

But here's the truth:

- Supplements won't fix poor diet or chronic stress.

- They are tools, not cures.
- Used correctly, they can accelerate healing, ease symptoms, and bridge nutritional gaps — but they shouldn't replace foundational habits.

Later in this book we will talk about each of our supplements and what they can help with. For me REZCUE was amazing at fixing inflammation caused by the various gut issues that I suffered with. As I've mentioned, since the root cause of those issues turned out to be low stomach acid, for me it was taking Triple HCL with meals that literally transformed my life. And without that external boost of a betaine HCL supplement, I think it would have been hard to get to where I am now (at least as quickly as I was able to!).

Final thoughts

True gut health comes from addressing the whole picture — not just popping a pill or cutting out a food group that you feel you are intolerant to. When you focus on these six core pillars, you create a strong foundation for long-lasting health, energy, and resilience.

You do not have to change lots of things in one go. In fact, I would advise against that because it just will not last. Going back to my personal training days, it was always the people who went "all in" in January that soon reverted back to their old habits. Just introducing one or two things each month (like a tweak to your diet or a walk after a meal). Once those have become part of your normal routine then you can add something else. Over the course of a year you will end up making serious progress that actually sticks and becomes normal, easy and fully integrated into your daily routine.

> ### 💡 Quick Tip: Focus on Your Sleep
>
> **Poor sleep affects your gut**, and poor gut health affects your sleep—it's a two-way street.
>
> Aim for **7–9 hours of restful sleep** each night to support gut repair and balance.
>
> I try and limit my screen time by putting my phone on charge early and **wear blue light blocking glasses when I'm watching TV**. A Magnesium Glycinate supplement really helps me too. Again, it works for me, but you need to find what works for you!

How Your Gut Works

The Journey of Digestion – From Entry to Exit

This chapter could honestly be a book on its own! But it's important that we have a solid foundation of understanding of the process if we're going to discuss ways that we can improve it.

Digestion is a complex yet beautifully orchestrated process that ensures our bodies receive the necessary nutrients to function. This journey begins the moment food enters your mouth and ends with waste elimination and involves multiple organs working in harmony. Let's go step-by-step through this incredible process.

1. The Mouth – Where Digestion Begins

It's easy to forget that the digestive process starts in the mouth, where food is broken down both mechanically and chemically. Teeth grind and chew food into smaller pieces, increasing the surface area for enzymes to act upon. Saliva, produced by the salivary glands, contains amylase, a crucial enzyme that begins breaking down carbohydrates. The tongue helps with mixing your food with saliva and shaping it into a mass of food that is called "bolus", which is then pushed to the back of the throat for swallowing. When you start to understand the complexity of what is going on in your mouth you appreciate why we have always been told to chew our food properly!

2. The Oesophagus – A Passageway to the Stomach

Once swallowed, the bolus travels down the oesophagus, a muscular tube that connects the mouth to the stomach. This movement is facilitated by a series of wave-like muscle contractions that push food downward (technically known as "peristalsis"). A critical structure at the lower end of the oesophagus is the lower oesophageal sphincter (LES), which opens to allow food into the stomach and closes to prevent acid reflux. A weakened LES can be an obvious cause for acid reflux and heartburn.

3. The Stomach – The Acidic Breakdown

The stomach of course plays a crucial role in digestion by secreting gastric juices, including hydrochloric acid (HCL) and more enzymes such as pepsin, which break down proteins. The stomach's muscular walls churn food, mixing it with these digestive secretions to form a semi-liquid substance called "chyme". Mucus lining the stomach protects it from its own acidic environment. Enzyme deficiency and / or low stomach acid can be common underlying issues for people's digestive issues.

4. The Small Intestine – Absorption Central

Chyme then leaves the stomach and enters the small intestine. This is where most digestion and nutrient absorption occurs. This amazing organ consists of three sections:

- **Duodenum**: The first segment, where digestive enzymes from the pancreas and bile from the liver aid in further breaking down fats, proteins, and carbohydrates.
- **Jejunum**: The middle section, where most nutrient absorption takes place.
- **Ileum**: The final section, where remaining nutrients are absorbed before passing into the large intestine.

The pancreas secretes all three of the crucial digestive enzymes; amylase, lipase, and protease. While bile from the liver helps emulsify fats, making them easier to digest and absorb. Bile also neutralises the hydrochloric acid and makes the chyme alkaline. This rapid change in the pH levels of the chyme (from very acidic to alkaline) greatly increases the digestion and absorbability of the nutrients.

5. The Large Intestine – Water Reabsorption and Waste Formation

After nutrients are absorbed, the remaining waste moves into the large intestine (commonly referred to as the colon although technically speaking they are not *exactly* the same thing!). Here, water and electrolytes are reabsorbed, and beneficial bacteria further break down undigested food particles, producing certain vitamins like Vitamin K. The large intestine also compacts waste into faeces.

6. The Rectum and Anus

Faeces is stored in the rectum until its ready to be eliminated. The process of defecation is controlled by both voluntary and involuntary muscles, ensuring waste is expelled efficiently.

The Role of Enzymes in Digestion

You might have noticed the crucial role that enzymes play in various stages of the digestive process. If you'd like to learn more about digestive enzymes, then I can highly recommend Joni's eBook "The Little Book of Enzymes" which is available as a free download on the THERA Nordic website. However, it's worth just highlighting the role and different types of digestive enzymes since they play such a vital role in breaking down food into absorbable nutrients. They are biological catalysts that speed up chemical reactions in digestion. Different enzymes target specific macronutrients:

- **Amylase** (found in saliva and pancreatic juice): Breaks down carbohydrates into simple sugars.
- **Protease** (such as pepsin in the stomach and trypsin from the pancreas): Digests proteins into amino acids.
- **Lipase** (produced in the pancreas): Aids in fat digestion by breaking down triglycerides into fatty acids and glycerol.

By improving digestion, enzymes help maximize nutrient absorption, reduce bloating, and support overall gut health. They are really amazing things!

The digestive system is an intricate network that transforms food into the essential nutrients our bodies need while efficiently eliminating waste. Each organ plays a vital role, ensuring that digestion is smooth and efficient, allowing us to maintain optimal health.

Now that you have a some understanding of the process we can start to delve into some common myths and then begin to look at how gut health impacts so many other parts of your overall wellbeing. Along the way hopefully there will be areas that you can better understand and relate to when it comes to working on your own gut health journey. The more we understand about why our body is behaving like it is the better chance we have of fixing the underlying problem.

> ### 💡 Quick Tip: Kiwi is a gut superfood!
>
> Kiwi's high fibre content helps to promote regular bowel movements and soften stools.
>
> It contains a natural digestive enzyme "actinidin", which helps break down protein (similar to the protease that your body produces)
>
> Consuming two kiwis before bedtime has been linked to improved sleep quality and duration, possibly due to its high antioxidant content and serotonin levels, which may help produce melatonin, the sleep hormone.

Common Gut Health Myths

When it comes to gut health, there's *a lot* of misinformation out there. Between social media trends, marketing gimmicks, and half-truths, it's easy to get caught up in advice that sounds good but isn't actually backed by science.

Let's clear up some of the biggest myths and set the record straight.

Myth 1: Probiotics Fix Everything

The Truth: Probiotics can be great, but they're *not* a magic cure for gut issues.

Probiotics are helpful bacteria, but they're not always the solution—especially if you're dealing with SIBO (Small Intestinal Bacterial Overgrowth), low stomach acid, or severe dysbiosis (an imbalance of gut bacteria). Taking the wrong strain, or too much, can sometimes make things worse!

What actually works?

Instead of blindly taking probiotics when you are not sure exactly what you are deficient in, focus on feeding your good gut bacteria with fibre, fermented foods (if tolerated), and a diverse diet full of as much colour as possible. If you do take probiotics, try to choose the right strain for you. For example,

"Saccharomyces boulardii" is often beneficial if you've had a stomach bug or diarrhea. There are microbiome tests available to see if you are deficient in certain strains, although these can vary in accuracy. The point is that you may need a more targeted approach for your body than just grabbing the nearest probiotic supplement. Later in this book we'll talk about the importance of getting enough *pre*biotic fibre to feed the good bacteria (your probiotics!), as this can often be a better approach.

Myth 2: You Need to Detox Regularly

The Truth: Your body is naturally detoxing *all the time*!

The liver, kidneys, and digestive system are constantly filtering and eliminating toxins. Juice cleanses, detox teas, and extreme fasting might make you feel lighter, but they're *not* necessary for real detoxification.

What actually works?

Supporting your body's natural detox pathways by:

- Eating fibre-rich foods to help your gut remove waste.
- Staying hydrated (water is the best "detox" drink there is!).
- Supporting your liver with nutrients from cruciferous veggies (broccoli, kale, cauliflower).
- Moving your body—sweating helps eliminate toxins too!

Myth 3: If You're Bloated, You Must Have Food Intolerances

The Truth: Bloating isn't *always* caused by food intolerances—it can be due to low stomach acid, poor digestion, or stress.

People often assume bloating means they need to cut out dairy, gluten, or other foods, but in many cases, bloating happens because:

- You're not breaking down your food properly due to low stomach acid or enzyme deficiencies.
- You're eating too fast, leading to trapped gas.
- Your gut bacteria are fermenting food in the wrong place (as is the case in SIBO).

What actually works?

- Eating slowly and chewing food properly.
- Supporting digestion with digestive enzymes or HCL if needed.
- Managing stress—since the gut and nervous system are deeply connected.
- Identifying *real* food intolerances through elimination diets or testing, rather than guessing.

Myth 4: Heartburn Means You Have Too Much Stomach Acid

The Truth: In many cases, heartburn can be caused by too little stomach acid, not too much.

This one surprises a lot of people! Low stomach acid (hypochlorhydria) can cause food to sit in the stomach for too long, leading to fermentation and bloating. Amongst other digestive issues, this can increase intra-abdominal pressure, causing the lower oesophageal sphincter (LES) to relax inappropriately, allowing stomach contents to reflux into the oesophagus, resulting in heartburn.

But instead of fixing the root cause, many people turn to antacids and PPIs (proton pump inhibitors), which lower stomach acid even more—making the problem worse in the long run. And not digesting your food properly, because your stomach acid is too low, can lead to a host of other problems. So, it really can become a negative spiral.

What actually works?

- Try supporting digestion with a betaine HCL supplement or apple cider vinegar before meals (if tolerated).

- Avoiding trigger foods, but more importantly, fixing digestion at the root.
- REZCUE can help to repair the inflammation in the gut lining that is caused by excessive acid reflux. This is a better way to sooth the pain, without taking medication that dilutes the stomach acid (which will sooth the pain but potentially make the underlying situation worse!).

Myth 5: Artificial Sweeteners Are Gut-Friendly Because They Have No Calories

The Truth: Many artificial sweeteners can disrupt gut bacteria and cause bloating.

While they might seem like a healthier alternative to sugar, sweeteners like aspartame, sucralose, and saccharin have been shown to negatively impact gut bacteria. Some (like sorbitol and maltitol) can also cause bloating and diarrhea in sensitive individuals.

What actually works?

- Choosing natural sweeteners like honey, maple syrup, or monk fruit in moderation.

- Opting for stevia or allulose, which are generally better tolerated.
- Focusing on reducing your overall sweet cravings instead of relying on replacements.

> ### 💡 Quick Tip: Watch Out for Common Triggers
>
> **Ultra-processed foods, excessive sugar, alcohol, and refined oils** can all disrupt gut health.
>
> Limit artificial sweeteners (like sucralose and aspartame), as they may harm beneficial bacteria.

Gut Health & Your Skin

Before founding THERA Nordic, I worked in the skincare industry for many years, treating clients in clinics, running my own practice, and helping people achieve healthy, glowing skin. I've seen firsthand how much money people are willing to spend on products, facials, and other treatments—desperately hoping for that flawless, youthful complexion. But over time, one thing became crystal clear to me; great skin doesn't start with what you put on your face—it starts with what's happening inside your body.

I used to have clients who did everything "right" when it came to skincare. They followed all the steps, used high-end products, and had regular treatments, but they still struggled with breakouts, redness, or dull, irritated skin. The moment I started looking deeper—at their gut health, digestion, and diet—the real changes started happening.

I saw people who had suffered with acne for years clear up their skin by fixing their digestion. I watched eczema and rosacea calm down when gut inflammation was addressed. And I realised that no cream, serum, or facial would ever match the power of healing from the inside out.

How Gut Issues Show Up on Your Skin

When your gut is thriving, your skin looks better. It's as simple as that. But when your gut is out of balance, your skin can start sending distress signals. Common skin issues that can be linked to poor gut health include:

1. Acne & Breakouts

- If your gut is inflamed, your skin will be too.
- A damaged gut lining (leaky gut) can trigger breakouts and redness.
- Sugar, processed food, and dairy can make it worse by feeding bad bacteria in the gut.

2. Dry, Dull Skin & Premature Aging

- If your gut isn't absorbing nutrients properly, your skin misses out on hydration, collagen, and antioxidants—all the good stuff that keeps it plump and glowing.
- Low stomach acid (which many people have without realising) makes it hard to absorb essential skin nutrients like zinc, iron and vitamin B12.

3. Eczema, Psoriasis & Rosacea

- Skin conditions like eczema and psoriasis almost always link back to gut health.
- If your gut bacteria is off balance (dysbiosis), it can cause flare-ups, redness, and irritation.
- People with rosacea often have SIBO (Small Intestinal Bacterial Overgrowth), which means their gut bacteria has overgrown in the wrong place.

4. Dark Circles & Puffy Eyes

- Poor digestion can overload your liver, which makes you look tired and puffy.
- If your liver is struggling to detox properly, toxins start showing up in your skin.

💡 Quick Tip: Don't Forget to Chew!

Digestion starts in the mouth. Chewing thoroughly breaks down food, making it easier to digest and absorb nutrients.

Aim to chew each bite **20–30 times** to a soft texture before swallowing.

Skincare from the Inside Out

If you're serious about your skin, you need to start with your gut. Here's are a few tips to get you started (and to make sure you are getting the most out of your existing skincare routine!):

1. Heal Your Gut First (then treat your skin)

- Eat more gut-healing foods like bone broth, sauerkraut, kimchi, and artichokes.
- Again, make sure your stomach acid is working properly (apple cider vinegar before meals can help).
- Cut back on processed foods and sugar —they fuel gut inflammation.

2. Be Kind to Your Skin's Microbiome

- Just like your gut, your skin has its own bacteria that protect it. Harsh cleansers and over-exfoliating can strip it away.
- Use gentle skincare that supports your skin barrier instead of wrecking it.
- Stop overloading on antibiotics (both topical and oral)—they kill the good bacteria your skin needs.

3. Get the Right Nutrients for Skin Health

Your skin relies on nutrients from your food—but if your gut isn't absorbing them properly, it won't make a difference. You need:

- Collagen & Vitamin C – For skin elasticity and repair. Bone broth can be a great source of collagen.
- Omega-3s – From fatty fish, walnuts, and flaxseeds to calm inflammation.
- Zinc – Crucial for clear skin and acne prevention.
- Prebiotic fibre – To support your gut microbiome and reduce breakouts. Daily Health Fibre is a great source if you need a boost, but we'll discuss fibre in more detail later in the book.
- Probiotics – These can certainly help if you are deficient. But, as we've already discussed, it can be hard to know what you should be taking without proper testing.

4. Manage Stress & Sleep Properly

- Stress messes up your gut, which messes up your skin—it's all connected.

- High cortisol (stress hormone) can cause oily skin, breakouts, and premature aging.
- Poor sleep affects your gut microbiome and increases inflammation—get 7-9 hours.

Bottom Line: Fix Your Gut, Fix Your Skin

If you've tried every skincare product under the sun and your skin still isn't happy, it's time to look deeper. The gut is where everything starts.

Instead of wasting money on another expensive cream, work on healing your digestion first. Once your gut is balanced, your skin will naturally become clearer, brighter, and healthier.

The best skincare routine? A healthy gut, real food, and less stress. You can spend all the money in the world on skincare, but if your gut isn't in check, you're wasting your time (and your bank balance).

How supplements can help your skin

It's worth pointing out that the entire THERA Nordic range can have a direct benefit to your skin. Here's a very brief overview of how each product would help. Please note that this is *not* to say that you should introduce the entire range as part of your skincare routine! Just that the products that support your personal gut issues may well have a positive impact on your skin too.

REZCUE – Repairs and protects the gut lining, reducing inflammation that can lead to acne, eczema, and irritation.

Triple HCL – Enhances digestion and nutrient absorption, ensuring your skin gets the hydration and nutrients it needs.

Optimized Enzymes – Breaks down food efficiently to reduce bloating and indigestion, preventing inflammatory skin reactions.

Move – Supports regular bowel movements and detoxification, eliminating toxins that could otherwise contribute to breakouts.

Daily Healthy Fibre – Feeds beneficial gut bacteria, promoting microbiome balance and reducing systemic inflammation.

Bacti-Balance – Helps maintain a healthy bacterial balance, supporting clear skin and preventing breakouts linked to bacterial imbalances.

Hormones & Gut Health

Many people battle with hormonal imbalances at different periods throughout their lives. And in many cases, we're not always aware that the issue we are struggling with is causing havoc with the balance of our hormones.

All of us will remember the trauma of going through puberty. Women can suffer with irregular periods, mood swings, stubborn weight gain, breakouts, and eventually perimenopause and menopause. Men can suffer with hormonal imbalance too, low testosterone being a common issue that is not helped by modern lifestyles. But testing hormone levels is not easy or even available for many people.

The gut and hormones are in constant communication, and when your gut health is poor, it can throw your entire hormonal system out of balance. Let's break down how this works and what you can do to support both your gut and hormones naturally.

How Poor Gut Health Affects Hormones

Your gut isn't just for digestion—it's actually one of the key regulators of hormones in your body. When your gut is struggling (due to poor diet, stress, inflammation, or an imbalance in gut bacteria), it can disrupt everything from women's menstrual cycles to your mood and metabolism.

The Gut-Hormone Feedback Loop

Your gut directly impacts hormone production, metabolism, and elimination. Here's how they influence each other:

- **Estrogen Balance** – Your gut is responsible for breaking down and eliminating excess estrogen. If your gut isn't functioning properly (e.g., due to constipation or dysbiosis), estrogen can recirculate in the body, leading to symptoms like PMS, heavy periods, bloating, and mood swings. But men can suffer from fluctuating estrogen too, with low estrogen levels often linked to low testosterone.
- **Cortisol & Stress** – Your gut and brain communicate through the gut-brain axis. When your gut is inflamed or imbalanced, it can trigger higher cortisol (the stress hormone), which can lead to anxiety, poor sleep, and weight gain—especially around the midsection.
- **Insulin & Blood Sugar** – The gut microbiome influences insulin sensitivity. If your gut is out of balance, it can contribute to blood sugar swings, cravings, and even conditions like PCOS (Polycystic Ovary Syndrome) in women.

- **Thyroid Function** – Although 60% of your thyroid hormone (T4) gets converted to its active form (T3) in the liver, around 20% is converted in the gut. If your gut health is poor, this conversion can be impaired, leading to symptoms like fatigue, weight gain, and sluggish metabolism.

Treating Common Hormonal Conditions with Better Gut Health

If you've ever struggled with any of these issues, gut health may be a major factor, so addressing these issues can be a great support in the treatment. Please note that I am not suggesting that gut health is a magic bullet to cure these conditions. It's important that you seek out support from the usual medical channels too. But focusing on your gut health can be a huge support for your body and play a key role in your recovery.

Whilst hormone fluctuations are more commonly discussed in relation to women, men can suffer from issues relating to hormone imbalances that are made worse by poor gut health too. So, the advice on how to improve your gut health can still be a huge benefit, even if you are not specifically suffering from the issues outlined in this chapter.

Menopause

During menopause, estrogen levels fluctuate, which can affect gut bacteria and slow digestion. Many women notice bloating, constipation, and changes in metabolism during this time. Since the gut plays a role in estrogen detoxification, a sluggish gut can lead to symptoms like hot flashes, brain fog, and weight gain.

Here are some common gut related symptoms that can be caused during menopause or perimenopause:

Bloating & Gas

Fluctuating estrogen levels can cause a reduction in cortisol, potentially leading to constipation, bloating, and gas. Fluctuating progesterone levels may slow gut movement, exacerbating bloating.

There are a number of things that you can try including:

- Identifying trigger foods
- Introduce regular aerobic exercise

- Consider herbal remedies
- Take a prebiotic fibre (like Daily Healthy Fibre)
- Use targeted supplements to boost your digestive health
- Staying hydrated is crucial

Constipation

The fluctuating estrogen and progesterone levels can also lead to constipation. To address constipation, looking at your diet is the first step. But consider these steps to help:

- Double your daily fibre intake
- Take the right fibre (grains, fruits, vegetables, nuts, and seeds are a great source of fibre)
- Consider supplementing your fibre
- Drink one more litre of water per day

Acid Reflux & Heartburn

During perimenopause and menopause, hormonal fluctuations can weaken the muscles, including the valve at the top of the stomach, which normally keeps stomach contents in place after eating.

Additionally, decreasing hormone levels often lead to reduced stomach acid production, which may be mistaken for over-acidity. This can exacerbate symptoms, as insufficient stomach acid fails to adequately break down meals, leading to fermentation and gas production, which in turn increases pressure on the stomach valve, causing acid reflux. In extreme cases this can lead to GERD (see below).

Gastroesophageal Reflux Disease (GERD)

Gastroesophageal Reflux Disease (GERD, or officially GORD in the UK) has a very clear connection to perimenopause and menopause.

- Symptoms include:
- Regular Acid Reflux
- Unpleasant Sour Taste in the Mouth
- Heartburn
- Trouble Swallowing
- Persistent Cough

How to Support Gut & Hormone Balance Naturally

Even if you are not struggling with the issues in this chapter, there are some general best practices that you can work into your daily routine to optimise your body's chances of keeping your hormones in balance:

- Prioritise Fibre: This helps to remove excess estrogen, supports digestion, and feeds beneficial gut bacteria. Great sources of fibre are from flaxseeds, chia seeds, leafy greens, oats, and cruciferous veggies (broccoli, cauliflower, Brussels sprouts).
- Support digestion by making sure you have good stomach acid levels (HCL). This helps break down food, absorb nutrients, and also helps to prevent bloating and other issues that come from not digesting your food properly. As well as a betaine HCL and digestive enzymes supplements, great ways to give your body a boost of HCL include apple cider vinegar and bitter greens.
- Support gut bacteria with fermented foods and probiotics.

- Stay hydrated to prevent sluggish digestion and bloating.

If you're struggling with hormonal symptoms—whether it's acne, PMS, irregular cycles, thyroid issues, or menopause symptoms—part of the answer may lie in your gut. The good news is that you can support hormone balance naturally by focusing on gut-friendly nutrition, reducing stress, and maintaining a healthy lifestyle.

💡 Quick Tip: Understand the Role of Enzymes

Digestive enzymes can support the breakdown of food, especially if digestion feels weak or sluggish.

Enzymes help with **protein, fat, and carbohydrate breakdown**, reducing bloating and supporting nutrient absorption.

Travel & Gut Health

I've always loved traveling, but if there's one thing I've learned, it's that jet lag, different time zones, changes in food, and disrupted routines can seriously throw off my gut. This is somewhat obvious given we've already talked about the strong link between good sleep and gut health. So, when I'm travelling, this is where I really need to be on top of my gut health, because without this focus, I really feel it. Very quickly I can notice bloating, sluggish digestion, and just generally feeling off my A-game!

When we travel, we're also often not eating the same foods, our meal timings can be all over the place (at least from the point of view of our body clock which will be working hard to adjust!), and let's be honest—sometimes we indulge a little more than usual (which we should, because life is for enjoying!). But I also know that when my gut is off, everything feels off. So over time, I've figured out a few things that help me stay on track while still enjoying the experience.

Why Travel Messes with Gut Health

1. **Time Zone Shifts & Jet Lag**: Our digestion works on a circadian rhythm, just like our sleep cycle. When we switch time zones, our digestive system takes a hit too. I notice this especially when flying long-haul—

my stomach feels sluggish, and I either end up bloated or irregular.

2. **Changes in Food & Water**: Even if I'm eating "healthy" options, my gut isn't used to the new food sources, water quality, or different oils and seasonings. This can lead to bloating, gas, or food sensitivities that I don't normally have.
3. **Disrupted Routine & Stress**: Travel is fun, but it's also tiring. With early wakeups, battling through the airports and different meal timings, my gut definitely notices the stress—even if I don't feel it mentally

How I Support My Gut While Traveling

These are the areas that I focus on (even more than usual!) when I'm travelling. Most of these are fairly generic and should work for everyone. But as we've talked about in this book, we are all different and our bodies will react to different external and internal factors in different ways. So have a go and see what works for you:

1. **I Stick to My Key Supplements**: I don't travel without my Triple HCL for my low stomach acid levels, as well as Daily Healthy Fibre and Move (to keep things moving). I also always take REZCUE

more when I travel in order to keep my inflammation and leaky gut under control. I carry Bacti-Balance in case I was to get an upset stomach or feel under the weather. Bacti-Balance is great for boosting immunity.

2. **I Stay Hydrated (But Watch the Water Source!):** Dehydration causes major problems for digestion, and airplanes can be very dehydrating. I always bring a reusable water bottle and make sure I drink as much as I can, but I'm also mindful of water quality in new places. If I'm somewhere where the tap water isn't great, I stick to bottled or filtered water to avoid unwanted gut issues. It's common advice but remember to watch out for the ice in your drink too since this is often made from tap water!

3. **I Time My Meals to Adjust Faster:** Instead of eating at random times (like grabbing something in the airport just to kill some time!), I try to get onto my destination's eating schedule as soon as possible. If I land in the morning, I'll have a proper breakfast instead of snacking on the plane.

4. **I Prioritise Fibre & Protein When I Can:** I want to enjoy myself when I travel (in fact that is my priority!), but I make sure to include gut-friendly foods when possible—like vegetables, lean proteins, and healthy fats. Too much sugar and processed food back-to-back always makes me feel worse.

5. **I Move (Even If It's Just Walking):** Sitting for long periods slows digestion. Whether it's stretching in my hotel room, taking the stairs instead of the lifts, or just walking as much as possible (often a better way of exploring new places), movement always helps my gut reset.

6. **I Manage Stress & Sleep:** If I'm sleep-deprived and running on adrenaline, my gut is the first thing to suffer. I make sure to get proper rest, and if I need to, I take magnesium at night to help me wind down and keep my digestion regular. When buying magnesium supplements, you'll notice that there are lots of different forms of magnesium. Magnesium Glycinate is best for sleep

Travel Is Meant to Be Enjoyed, Not Stressful

At the end of the day, I don't stress too much about food while traveling—I love experiencing new places and cultures! But I also know that when my gut is happy, I enjoy the trip much more. So, I do what I can to support my digestion, without being overly restrictive. Because let's be honest, sometimes you just need to enjoy the croissant in Paris or the street food in Vietnam without overthinking it.

💡 Quick Tip: Manage Stress

Chronic stress is a major gut disruptor. It weakens digestion, alters gut bacteria, and can worsen IBS, reflux, and more.

Try daily practices like **deep breathing, meditation, yoga, nature walks, or journaling**—even **5 minutes a day** can make a difference.

The Critical Role of Fibre

When people think about gut health, fibre is often one of the first things that comes to mind—and for good reason! Fibre is one of the most essential nutrients for maintaining a healthy, balanced digestive system, yet many people don't fully understand what it does, why it matters, and how it works in the body.

What Is Fibre?

Fibre is the part of plant foods, like fruits, vegetables, grains, legumes, nuts, and seeds that your body can't fully digest. Unlike fats, proteins, and carbohydrates that your body breaks down and absorbs, fibre passes through the digestive system largely intact, but along the way, it plays a powerful role.

> ### 💡 Quick Tip: Focus on Balancing your Fibre
>
> Too much fibre too quickly can backfire, causing more bloating and discomfort.
>
> Introduce fibre gradually and adjust based on your body's signals—what works for one person may not work for another.

The Different Types of Fibre

1. **Soluble fibre:** This type of fibre dissolves in water to form a gel-like substance. It helps to slow digestion and can stabilise blood sugar levels and cholesterol.
   Found in: Oats, flaxseeds, psyllium husk, apples, and beans.
2. **Insoluble fibre:** This type of fibre adds bulk to stool and helps food move more efficiently through the digestive tract, preventing constipation.
   Found in: whole grains, nuts, seeds, and the skins of fruits and vegetables.

Prebiotic fibre

These are specific types of fibre that feed the good bacteria in your gut helping them grow and thrive (referred to as a *prebiotic* effect as it supports your body's *probiotics*). These bacteria are essential for immune function, mood regulation, and digestion. Most (but not all!) sources of prebiotic fibre are soluble. But not all soluble fibre has a prebiotic effect.
Found in: foods like garlic, onions, leeks, asparagus, bananas, and chicory root. THERA Nordic's Daily Healthy Fibre is a great source of soluble, prebiotic fibre if you need a boost.

Understanding the prebiotic effect of fibre is really key. Many people go straight to a probiotic (potentially for a strain of bacteria that they don't actually need!) before using a *pre*biotic fibre to nourish the *pro*biotics that you already have.

Why Is Fibre So Important?

1. It Nourishes Your Gut Microbiome

Your gut is home to trillions of bacteria—some good, some bad. Fibre is the primary food source for the beneficial bacteria in your gut. When these bacteria "eat" fibre (especially prebiotic fibre), they produce short-chain fatty acids (SCFAs) like butyrate, which can help to:

- Reduce inflammation in the gut.
- Strengthen the gut lining, preventing "leaky gut".
- Support immune function and reduce the risk of disease.

A well-fed microbiome is crucial for overall health, including digestion, brain health, and immunity.

2. It Supports Regular, Healthy Bowel Movements

Insoluble fibre adds bulk to stool and helps keep things moving, preventing constipation and promoting regularity. Without enough fibre, stools can become hard and difficult to pass, or too loose and watery if the gut is imbalanced.

3. It Helps Prevent "Hidden Constipation" and Bloating

Interestingly, many people who experience loose stools or diarrhea may actually be constipated—with impacted material in the bowel causing "overflow diarrhea". Fibre helps regulate this by bulking up stools and clearing out the colon, reducing bloating and discomfort.

4. It Regulates Blood Sugar and Energy

Soluble fibre slows the absorption of sugars into the bloodstream, preventing spikes and crashes in blood sugar. This leads to more stable energy and reduces the strain on insulin, which is vital for metabolic health.

5. It Supports Weight Management and Satiety

Fibre adds volume to meals without adding calories, helping you feel full and satisfied for longer. This can reduce overeating and cravings, supporting healthy weight management naturally.

6. It Detoxifies the Body

Fibre binds to waste products, toxins, excess hormones (like estrogen), and cholesterol, helping to carry them safely out of the body. This is essential for hormone balance, liver health, and reducing toxic load.

Why Are We Not Getting Enough?

Modern diets, heavy in processed foods and low in whole plants, are severely lacking in fibre. Most people get less than half the recommended daily amount, which is about 25–30 grams per day for adults.

Without enough fibre:

- Gut bacteria starve, reducing beneficial species.
- Digestion slows down, leading to constipation or irregularity.
- Inflammation in the gut may increase.
- Risk of chronic diseases like diabetes, heart disease, and colon cancer rises.

How to Start Adding More Fibre (Gently!)

Important: If you're not used to eating fibre, go slow! Adding too much too quickly can cause bloating, gas, and discomfort.

3. Start with small amounts of fibre-rich foods and gradually increase. At the start of this chapter there are the examples of soluble, insoluble and prebiotic fibre. Try and start to add as many of those into your diet as you can. Many of them make great, healthier

- alternatives to snacks in the cupboard or ingredients for a smoothy.
- Drink plenty of water to help fibre move smoothly through the gut.
- Consider prebiotic blends like Daily Healthy Fibre, which combine gentle fibres like Acacia and PHGG that are well-tolerated even by sensitive guts.

Final Thought: Fibre as a Foundation for Gut Health

Fibre isn't just about going to the toilet—it's about building a resilient, balanced gut environment that supports your whole body. From immunity to mood, weight to hormone balance, fibre is one of the simplest yet most powerful tools for health.

If you're working on healing your gut, fibre should be part of that journey—introduced carefully, adapted to your unique needs, and always alongside other lifestyle and dietary changes that support long-term wellbeing.

Gut Health Advice for Parents

Running a business is rewarding but can be tough at times, and I have setup and run a few over the years. But by far the most difficult job I have had was being a parent. My girls are now 17 and 19 and, like all Mums, I'm incredibly proud of them. Both are very into their sport (which really helps to keep teenagers on the right path!) and both of them are really good with their nutrition. My eldest is off to America on an athletics scholarship this year and takes her diet very seriously alongside her physical training.

Like all parents, I've made plenty of mistakes along the way. There is no instruction manual and the advice that is available for parents today is probably more confusing and contradictory than the world of gut health and nutrition! One area that you perhaps won't be surprised to hear was a focus for me (since they were babies!) is their nutrition. It can be hard at times and the availability and temptation for convenient, fast options is overwhelming. But it's been amazing to see that by putting the effort in with their diet they have now developed preferences for more healthy options. At their ages I've of course had to learn to let them make their own independent choices about what they want to eat, and it's interesting to see that, given the choice, they just won't eat much chocolate, sweets or fast food. We're not born with those addictions and cravings, but the availability of processed foods and high-sugar foods in society shapes our palettes and our choices and behaviours as adults.

So, the more you can help your children on their own gut journey, and the earlier you can start, the more you'll set them on a great path for a healthy life.

The Dangers of Processed Kids' Foods

I've always been cautious about processed foods. Foods packed with refined sugars, artificial additives, and preservatives can disrupt the balance of good bacteria in the gut. When consumed regularly, these foods can lead to issues like bloating, gas, irritability, and even skin breakouts.

The real danger is that many processed kids' foods, like sugary cereals, granola bars, and snacks, are marketed as being "healthy" when they often contain more sugar, additives, and refined grains than they do beneficial nutrients.

Better Snack Alternatives

Opting for whole-food snacks that are easy for kids to grab and go can still be just as fun as processed options, and so much better for their gut! Here are a few ideas that I used a lot when the girls were younger:

- Homemade energy balls with oats, nut butter, and chia seeds. I would often make a batch at the weekend and put them in the freezer. The kids used to love them!

- Vegetable sticks (peppers or carrots are great) with hummus or a homemade yogurt dip are super easy to chuck out if the kids are hungry.

- Mini whole-grain wraps with turkey or chicken and avocado are still popular in our house. Most kids love a chicken wrap, and it's a great way to get some healthy food inside them.

- Fruit kababs with berries, melon, or apples and a sprinkle of cinnamon. These are obviously still fairly high in sugar, so be mindful of that, but at least they are coming with all the fibre and other nutrients that you don't get in sugary, refined snacks for kids.

- Smoothie popsicles made with real fruit and yogurt

- Mini Avocado Toasts: Spread mashed avocado on whole grain toast and cut into small pieces. Kids love the creamy texture, and it's loaded with healthy fats and fibre.

- Apple Slices with Almond Butter: This is a classic snack—apple slices are fibre-rich, and almond butter provides healthy fats and protein, making this snack both delicious and satisfying.

- Veggie Muffins: You can sneak in veggies like carrots and zucchini into whole-grain muffins. Add some chia seeds or flaxseeds for a fibre boost. These are perfect for school lunches!

I've included some of these snacks in the appendix at the end of this book which contains a number of common recipes that I've relied on over the years.

Simple, Kid-Approved High-Fibre Meals

As much as I prioritise fibre in our household, I know that it's often a struggle to get kids to eat enough of it! The good news is that there are lots of fun ways to make fibre-rich foods enjoyable for your kids.

Here are some of my go-to high-fibre meals and that went down well with my kids:

Fibre-Rich Breakfasts

- Oatmeal with Berries and Chia Seeds: Oats are an excellent source of soluble fibre, and chia seeds add a bonus of omega-3s and even more fibre. Top with a few berries (antioxidant powerhouses) and a drizzle of honey for a sweet start to the day. Option to add Daily Healthy Fibre.

- Sourdough, smashed avocado and poached eggs. I love to also know that my kids have had a good protein source, and eggs are great for that.

- Smoothie Bowls: You can sneak a lot of fibre into smoothie bowls. Blend up some spinach, banana, flaxseeds, and almond milk, and top with granola, coconut flakes, and chia seeds for extra crunch and fibre. Again, as an option you could add Daily Healthy Fibre.

- Greek yogurt with berries, nut & seeds and a drop of honey. (one of my favorites)

Kid-Friendly Fibre-Filled Lunches & Dinners

- Homemade Chicken or Veggie Tacos: Use whole-grain tortillas for added fibre, and fill them with chopped veggies, grilled chicken, and a dollop of avocado or guacamole. This is a great meal to get them to enjoy fibre from the tortillas, veggies, and healthy fats.

- Sweet Potato and Black Bean Quesadillas: The natural sweetness of sweet potatoes is a big hit with kids, and combined with fibre-rich black beans, you have a meal that is both satisfying and gut-friendly.

- Veggie-Packed Pizzas: Use a whole wheat or cauliflower crust for extra fibre, and load the pizza up with tomatoes, spinach, zucchini, and bell peppers. Add a sprinkle of cheese and olive oil for healthy fat, and you've got a meal that's both fun and nutritious.

Tips for Getting Kids to Love Fibre:

- **Incorporate fibre gradually:** When introducing high-fibre foods, do it gradually to avoid digestive discomfort. Increasing fibre too quickly can lead to bloating and gas, so start slow and give their gut time to adjust.
- **Make Meals Colourful and Fun:** Kids love anything that looks fun! Use brightly coloured vegetables, fruits, and even fun-shaped cookie cutters to make their meals more appealing.
- **Sneak in Fibre:** If they're reluctant to eat certain foods, you can sneak in fibre by adding small amounts of ground flaxseeds, chia seeds, or ground oats into smoothies, pancakes, or baked goods. And of course, Daily Healthy Fibre.
- **Educate and Get Them Involved:** Whenever possible, I involve my daughters in meal prep. They love helping pick out veggies, helping prepare meals, and even creating their own meals. When they feel

like they're part of the process, they're much more likely to eat what's on their plate!

Gut Health Benefits for Kids

Gut health in kids is linked to much more than just digestion. A healthy microbiome in your kids can:

- **Boost Immunity:** A well-balanced gut supports a strong immune system, helping kids fight off infections.

- **Enhance Mood and Behaviour:** A healthy gut can positively impact mood, emotional regulation, and behaviour. Kids with gut imbalances may show more irritability or anxiety, so supporting their microbiome can contribute to a more stable mood. As parents we're all familiar with sugar spikes causing kids to go a little crazy, followed by the inevitable crash in mood.
- **Improve Skin Health:** As we've discussed, good gut health is key to clear, healthy skin. If your child suffers from conditions like eczema or acne, it may be linked to gut imbalances. Supporting gut health can reduce inflammation and promote clearer skin.

- **Help with Sleep:** Gut health and sleep are connected—if your child's digestive system is in balance, they're more likely to get restful, quality sleep.

By focusing on nurturing your child's gut health from a young age, you're setting them up for long-term health benefits. Healthy gut habits, balanced meals, and fibre-rich snacks can positively affect their digestion, immunity, skin, and even their mood. Ultimately, a healthy gut leads to a healthier, happier child!

> ### 💡 Quick Tip: Double your efforts after a course of anti-biotics
>
> Anti-biotics are a miracle of modern science but **remember that they kill off a lot of the good bacteria in the gut too.** Try to focus on your child's gut health even more if they have had a course of anti-biotics.

Mental Health & Gut Health: The Hidden Connection

I've always known that stress plays a massive role in gut health, but the more I've learned, the clearer it's become—your gut and brain are intricately connected. If my gut health is off, my mood follows. If I'm feeling anxious, I feel it in my stomach. It's a two-way street, and once you start paying attention, you realise just how much your digestion and mental state influence each other.

This connection is called the gut-brain axis, and many clinical studies are now proving that our gut health directly impacts mood, anxiety, stress, focus, and even depression. Your gut isn't just digesting food—it's constantly communicating with your brain, sending signals that can either keep you feeling calm and balanced or leave you feeling on edge, foggy, or low.

The Gut-Brain Axis: How Your Gut Talks to Your Brain

Your gut is often called your "second brain" because it has its own nervous system, called the enteric nervous system, which sends messages to the brain via the vagus nerve. Around 90% of serotonin (your "feel-good" neurotransmitter) and 50% of dopamine (which affects motivation and pleasure) are actually produced in your gut!

So, if your gut bacteria are out of balance (for example, too much bad bacteria, not enough diversity, or inflammation in the gut), your brain feels it directly. Studies show that poor gut health can contribute to:

- **Anxiety & Depression:** Imbalanced gut bacteria can reduce serotonin and dopamine production, which directly affects mood.
- **Brain Fog & Poor Focus:** If your gut is inflamed, it can cause inflammation in the brain, leading to mental fatigue.
- **Increased Stress Response:** A healthy gut helps regulate cortisol (the stress hormone). An unhealthy gut can make you more prone to chronic stress.

Foods That Support Mood & Mental Clarity

One of the easiest ways to support mental health is through food. Your gut bacteria thrive on nutrient-dense, whole foods that help balance neurotransmitters and keep inflammation low.

Foods that boost serotonin & dopamine naturally:

- **Tryptophan-rich foods**: Turkey, chicken, eggs, salmon, and nuts help produce serotonin.

- **Omega-3s:** Found in fatty fish (salmon, sardines) and flaxseeds, they reduce brain inflammation and support mood.
- **Fermented foods:** Yogurt, kimchi, sauerkraut, and kefir contain probiotics that enhance gut bacteria and neurotransmitter production.
- **Dark leafy greens:** Spinach, kale, and Swiss chard provide folate, which is essential for dopamine production.
- **High-fibre foods:** Whole grains, lentils, beans, and berries feed gut bacteria and stabilise blood sugar, preventing energy crashes.

You'll no doubt notice some common themes throughout the book. Since your gut is connected to, and directly feeds, so many systems within your body, the types of food that can help improve your mental state have many of the other benefits that we've talked about already.

Foods that can negatively impact mood & gut health:

- **Processed sugars and refined carbs:** These cause blood sugar spikes, which can trigger anxiety.
- **Artificial sweeteners:** These disrupt gut bacteria, which can affect neurotransmitter production.
- **Excess alcohol:** Alcohol damages the gut lining and alters brain chemistry.

How Gut Health Impacts Sleep & Focus

Good gut health doesn't just make you feel happier—it also helps you sleep better and stay mentally sharp.

When your gut bacteria are balanced, your body naturally produces more serotonin and melatonin, which help regulate sleep cycles. Poor gut health can lead to insomnia, restless sleep, or waking up feeling exhausted.

Your brain relies on a steady supply of nutrients from your gut. If your digestion is sluggish or inflamed, it can lead to brain fog, forgetfulness, and difficulty concentrating.

Finally, I want to re-emphasise that this is not a magic bullet, or a one size fits all solution to mental health. Mental health is a complex area and certainly beyond my area of expertise. The purpose of this chapter was simply to highlight the growing body of scientific evidence that points to the importance of the Gut-Brain axis, and how focusing on your nutrition can be so important for your mental health.

> ### 💡 Quick Tip: Consider Probiotics and Prebiotics
>
> Probiotics can help, but **they are not one-size-fits-all**—start low and go slow.
>
> Prebiotic fibres feed good bacteria but may need to be introduced carefully if sensitive.

The Future of Gut Health

As our understanding of the gut deepens, we are entering a truly exciting era of wellness. The science surrounding gut health is evolving rapidly, revealing just how crucial our gut microbiome is in not only digestive health but also disease prevention, longevity, and even mental well-being. We're just scratching the surface of what the gut microbiome can do, and new discoveries are being made almost daily.

The Role of the Gut Microbiome in Disease Prevention

One of the most promising areas of gut health research is the role the microbiome plays in preventing various diseases. The microbes in our gut don't just help with digestion—they influence our immune system, regulate inflammation, and can even play a role in preventing chronic diseases. Here's a quick look at how our gut might support our health, based on some of the most recent scientific studies:

- **Immune Function:** A healthy gut microbiome supports a strong immune system. About 70% of your immune cells are located in your gut, and your gut bacteria help regulate your immune response. A well-balanced microbiome can help prevent autoimmune diseases and chronic inflammation, while an imbalance (dysbiosis) can lead to conditions like inflammatory bowel disease (IBD), rheumatoid arthritis, and has been linked to various allergies.

- **Metabolic Health:** Research has shown that a healthy microbiome can prevent or help manage metabolic disorders such as obesity, type 2 diabetes, and insulin resistance. Gut bacteria influence how we metabolise fats and carbohydrates and help regulate fat storage. The balance between "good" and "bad" bacteria can make all the difference in preventing metabolic diseases.
- **Cardiovascular Health:** Emerging research indicates that gut health may also impact cardiovascular health. Studies have linked dysbiosis with an increased risk of hypertension, atherosclerosis, and heart disease. Gut bacteria produce certain metabolites (like short-chain fatty acids) that help regulate blood pressure and inflammation, showing that the heart and gut are more connected than we thought.

How Gut Health Affects Longevity

The idea that gut health can influence longevity is a fascinating area of study. As we learn more about the relationship between gut microbes and the aging process, it's becoming clear that our gut bacteria may play a critical role in how long (and how well!) we live. Here are some of the key reasons that scientists now believe that strong gut health could improve your lifespan:

- **Gut Microbes and Aging:** The diversity of your gut microbiome decreases as you age, and this loss of diversity has been linked to many age-related health conditions, including cognitive decline, frailty, and cardiovascular disease. Interestingly, research has shown that people who live longer and age more healthily tend to have more diverse and balanced gut microbiomes.
- **Cellular Aging:** Your gut also plays a role in cellular health. It has been shown that a well-balanced gut microbiome helps reduce inflammation, which is a major contributor to the aging process. Chronic inflammation, often referred to as "inflammaging" is linked to a variety of age-related diseases, from heart disease to Alzheimer's. By maintaining your

gut health, you can potentially slow down the biological effects of aging.
- **Mitochondrial Health:** Gut health influences the health of mitochondria, which are the powerhouses of our cells. Mitochondrial function is essential for energy production and overall cell health. Research is starting to show that the gut microbiome may affect mitochondrial function and efficiency, suggesting that a healthy gut could contribute to higher energy levels and improved cellular repair mechanisms as we age.

Latest Trends in Gut Health

The gut health field is evolving rapidly, and with it, new trends and exciting discoveries. Some of the latest innovations and trends in gut health include:

- **Postbiotics:** We've talked a little about probiotics (live beneficial bacteria) and prebiotics (fibre that feeds good bacteria), but now there's a growing interest in *postbiotics*—the byproducts or metabolites produced by probiotics as they interact with the gut. These postbiotics, like short-chain fatty acids (SCFAs), have powerful anti-inflammatory properties and have been shown to help improve gut integrity, reduce gut permeability (often referred to as "leaky gut"), and even support immune health. Postbiotics are being researched as a potential therapeutic option for a variety of gut-related conditions, and they may become a significant tool in maintaining gut health.

- **Psychobiotics:** As we learnt in the previous chapter, mental health and gut health have always been closely linked, and now the term "psychobiotics" is gaining traction. Psychobiotics refer to probiotics and prebiotics that can have a positive impact on mental health, such as reducing symptoms of anxiety, depression, and stress. Research suggests that certain strains of probiotics can influence the gut-brain axis, the communication system between the gut and the brain, helping to improve mood, reduce anxiety, and even increase feelings of happiness. As we continue to explore this field, psychobiotics may emerge as a go-to treatment for mental health disorders.

- **Fecal Microbiota Transplantation (FMT):** Although still a relatively new and developing therapy, FMT involves transplanting fecal matter from a healthy person into the digestive tract of someone with a gut-related condition. It has shown promising results in treating potentially life-threatening conditions like Clostridium difficile infections and could be used to treat other conditions like IBD or autoimmune diseases in the future. While not something that's on the horizon for everyday gut health, the potential applications of FMT in treating chronic gut issues are incredibly exciting.

- **Personalised Gut Health:** With advancements in genomics and microbiome sequencing, we're entering an era where gut health advice can be more personalised than ever before. Personalised gut health means that instead of general recommendations, we can look at an individual's specific microbiome to tailor dietary advice, supplements, and treatments. As more research emerges, it's likely that we'll see personalised gut health plans become more mainstream, helping people optimise their gut health based on their unique microbiome.

The ZOE Project

One area that I have been following for a number of years are the groundbreaking studies that are coming out from the ZOE Project, the world's largest personalised nutrition study. These have shown that gut microbiome diversity is one of the most powerful predictors of overall health and the importance of fibre in feeding the microbiome. This research was certainly one of the driving factors for us wanting to develop Daily Healthy Fibre, a high-quality prebiotic fibre.

The ZOE research has shown that people who consume a diverse range of fibre-rich, plant-based foods tend to have higher gut microbiome diversity, which is associated with:

- Reduced risk of chronic diseases (like type 2 diabetes and heart disease).
- Lower inflammation levels.
- Healthier weight and better metabolic health.
- Improved immune resilience.

As Professor Tim Spector says, "*The more diverse your diet, especially plant-based foods, the more diverse your gut microbiome—and that's the key to long-term health.*"

Dr. Will Bulsiewicz, author of *Fibre Fueled* (a book that has had a major influence on my journey) has also emphasised that fibre is essential for gut bacteria to thrive and produce short-chain fatty acids (SCFAs)—compounds that help heal the gut lining, reduce inflammation, and even improve brain health.

Why Modern Diets Fall Short

As we discussed in the chapter on fibre, modern processed diets are extremely low in fibre, especially the diverse plant fibres needed for microbiome health, with most people consuming less than half the recommended daily fibre intake (which is about 25–30g for adults). Without enough fibre:

- Good gut bacteria starve, and harmful bacteria can take over.
- Gut inflammation and "leaky gut" may develop.
- Digestion slows, leading to constipation and discomfort.
- The risk of chronic diseases rises.

Fibre is not just for digestion—it's the foundation of your entire gut ecosystem. It feeds the good bacteria that protect you from disease, regulate your mood, balance your hormones, and keep inflammation at bay.

As the ZOE Project and leading gut experts like Tim Spector and Dr. Will Bulsiewicz continue to show, real, lasting health starts with nourishing your microbiome—and fibre is the key to that nourishment.

So, if there's one thing to focus on for your gut health, let it be this: love your gut with fibre, and your gut will love you back.

The Future is Bright

It's clear that the future of gut health is bright, with new research and trends pointing toward innovative treatments, deeper understanding, and more personalised approaches to maintaining optimal gut health. Whether it's through postbiotics, psychobiotics, or even microbiome-based therapies, the next few years could change how we view and treat gut-related diseases, aging, and mental health.

As we learn more, one thing is for certain; gut health will continue to be a cornerstone of overall well-being. Whether you're looking to prevent disease, slow the aging process, or improve your mental clarity, caring for your gut should be at the top of your health priorities. Keep an eye on the exciting developments in this field—the future of gut health is evolving, and we're all part of the journey!

💡 Quick Tip: Eat a Diverse, Whole-Food Diet

Variety is key—the more diverse your diet, the more diverse your gut microbiome. Aim to "eat the rainbow" with plenty of colourful fruits and vegetables.

Include fermented foods like sauerkraut, kimchi, kefir, and yogurt (if tolerated) for natural probiotics.

Prioritise fibre—prebiotic fibres like oats, flaxseeds, chia seeds, and resistant starches (like cooked and cooled potatoes and rice) feed good bacteria.

Client Stories

Introduction

These are real stories from real clients that we have worked with at THERA Nordic. We have changed the names and any details that would identify the individual. I hope that their stories and their journey to better gut health give you hope that you can solve your own issues. We are here to help if we can!

Emily's Battle with Her Gut

Symptoms: Bloating, Indigestion, IBS

Emily had always considered herself a healthy person. She ate well, exercised regularly, and tried to maintain a balanced lifestyle. But for as long as she could remember, her stomach had been her greatest enemy. It started in her early twenties—random bloating after meals, discomfort that lingered for hours, and an unpredictable digestive system that seemed to have a mind of its own.

At first, she brushed it off. "Probably just something I ate," she would tell herself. But as the months turned into years, the issues became harder to ignore. One day, she'd feel completely backed up, sluggish, and uncomfortable, and the next, she'd be running to the bathroom with cramps so sharp they left her breathless. No pattern, no predictability—just frustration.

Doctors called it IBS and suggested eliminating certain foods. So, Emily tried. Dairy went first, then gluten. She cut out coffee, sugar, even some fruits. At one point, she was living off plain chicken and steamed vegetables. But nothing worked for long. Some days were better than others, but the relief never lasted.

Probiotics? She tried most of the major brands. Prescription medications? Some would provide some short-term relief but ultimately these seemed to make things worse. Every new supplement or dietary change brought hope, followed by disappointment. Social events became stressful—would this meal set her off? Would she have to leave early, clutching her stomach in pain?

Then came the exhaustion. Gut problems weren't just about digestion anymore. Emily felt drained, foggy, like her body was always fighting an invisible battle. She struggled to focus at work, her mood was all over the place, and anxiety over food made her hesitant to eat at all.

How we helped

I recognised some of her symptoms in my own story so the first thing I did was support her digestion with Triple HCL to help her break down food properly. Then, we focused on healing her gut lining with REZCUE and boosted her fibre intake with Daily Healthy Fibre.

I had her take a step back from restrictive dieting and instead focus on real, nourishing foods. To get her gut moving regularly, we introduced Move to help her bowel mobility.

Stress was a big factor too, so I suggested she worked on simple relaxation techniques to calm her nervous system. Within weeks, her bloating eased, her energy improved, and for the first time in years, she felt like herself again.

"I was constantly tired, bloated, and fed up with trying different things that never worked. THERA Nordic's products honestly turned things around—my gut feels calm and my energy's finally back. The care and support shown by Emma and Joni was something no other company has ever shown"

- Emily

Anna's Story: A Journey with MS, Major Surgery, and Ongoing Struggles

Symptoms: Bloating, constipation, gut inflammation from surgery

Anna is a woman in her early 50s who has lived with Multiple Sclerosis (MS) for over a decade. Like many with MS, she has faced her fair share of physical challenges, but nothing prepared her for the gut issues that would later take over her life.

A few years ago, due to severe complications with her digestive system, Anna underwent major surgery to remove half of her bowel. The hope was that this would bring some relief from the relentless pain, bloating, and constipation she had been facing. But even after such an extreme measure, her gut problems did not end.

Instead, Anna began to experience ongoing bleeding, often accompanied by severe discomfort and unpredictable digestion. Every meal became a question mark—would this cause a flare-up? Was she absorbing any nutrients at all? The bleeding in particular left her deeply worried and exhausted.

On top of all of this, managing MS symptoms required her to maintain as much stability in her body as possible, but how could she when her digestive system was in constant distress?

How we helped

Desperate for answers, Anna reached out to us, asking if there was anything—any supplement, any solution—that could help her heal. She explained her MS, her surgery, and the persistent bleeding.

I listened to Anna's story, and while we have many products designed to support gut healing and reduce inflammation, it was vital to be clear with her. When there is ongoing bleeding, especially in the context of major bowel surgery and a complex condition like MS, it is essential to work closely with a healthcare professional—ideally a gastroenterologist or a specialist familiar with her full medical history.

We explained that no supplement can or should be used to replace professional medical evaluation in a case like hers. Bleeding could indicate serious ongoing damage, ulceration, or other complications that require medical diagnosis and treatment—something that even the best-targeted nutritional products cannot resolve alone.

However, her doctor agreed that it was safe and appropriate for her to explore gentle support to help soothe her gut lining and tackle the inflammation that she could start to take REZCUE.

Anna appreciated the honesty and care in the response. She shared that, while she had been hesitant to return to hospital settings, she now felt empowered to seek the right help—knowing that supporting her body fully meant combining medical care with thoughtful, professional supplementations and a helpful nutrition plan. Whilst it is still early days, she feels that the REZCUE is having a major impact on her gut health and improving her day-to-day quality of life.

> *"After surgery, my gut was a mess, and nothing helped until I gave REZCUE a go. It really helped ease the pain and inflammation—I feel so much more comfortable now."*
>
> *- Anna*

Mark's Story: Living with Severe Acid Reflux

Symptoms: Acid reflux, Heartburn, Sore Throat

Mark is a 45-year-old father of two who never thought he would be afraid of eating. But for the past three years, he has been battling severe acid reflux that has completely turned his life upside down.

What started as occasional heartburn quickly escalated into daily episodes of burning pain, regurgitation of stomach acid, and a constant sore throat. The acid reflux became so severe that Mark would wake up in the middle of the night choking on acid, unable to sleep properly and exhausted by morning.

Doctors prescribed proton pump inhibitors (PPIs), which gave some temporary relief but never fully resolved the issue. Worse, Mark noticed that after months on PPIs, his digestion felt even weaker—he was bloated, gassy, and often constipated. He started to wonder if suppressing his stomach acid was actually making things worse

How we helped

In frustration, Mark reached out to us, asking if there was a natural way to heal his reflux and get his life back.

After hearing Mark's story and reassured him that he wasn't alone—many people face similar struggles, and there are steps that can support healing. But we also explained something important:

When acid reflux is severe—especially if it leads to nighttime choking, throat issues, or breathing symptoms—it's critical to continue working with a healthcare professional to rule out more serious conditions like Barrett's esophagus or severe esophageal damage.

I explained to Mark that there are ways to support his gut lining naturally, such as REZCUE to help soothe and repair the esophageal and stomach lining, and Triple HCL to address the possibility of low stomach acid, which paradoxically can be a root cause of reflux in many people (and why common medicines for short-term relief can make the problem worse because they dilute the stomach acid).

I also advised that when starting out with REZCUE, it is important to take it with food or in smaller doses if reflux is very active, so as not to aggravate symptoms initially.

Mark appreciated the balanced advice. For the first time, he felt like someone understood the full picture, and he was motivated to take the right steps to heal properly, not just suppress symptoms.

Within a few weeks Mark felt like his life had changed. The REZCUE soothed his sore throat, very quickly providing relief. He was able to come off the PPIs after a few weeks and his acid reflux and heartburn has now been almost completely eliminated. When Mark does have another flare up, he knows that he has the tools to deal with it.

> *"I used to wake up every night with reflux, even on meds. Since starting REZCUE and Triple HCL, I've been off the PPIs and sleeping properly again—total relief. I could not have understood the process without the guidance Emma gave me."* - Mark

Sophie's Story: The Hidden Constipation She Never Knew She Had

Symptoms: Constipation (but presenting with diarrhea)

Sophie, a woman in her late 30s, had been struggling with digestive issues for years—but she never once thought of herself as someone who was constipated. In fact, if you had asked her, she would have said the opposite:

But underneath the surface, Sophie's body was telling a very different story.

Her daily routine was dominated by urgency, unpredictable bowel movements, bloating, and constant discomfort. She felt like her digestion was "out of control." She also noticed her stomach was always distended, and she often felt full even after small meals.

How we helped

When Sophie finally reached out to us, she described her symptoms in detail—frequent loose stools, bloating, cramping, and the occasional sharp pain. She wanted to know if something like REZCUE could help calm her gut.

After listening to her story, one thing stood out: despite having watery stools, all the signs pointed to a classic case of "hidden constipation"—what's known medically as *"overflow diarrhea"*.

I explained to Sophie that sometimes when the bowel is backed up with impacted stool, only watery material can pass around it. So, although she was going to the toilet daily, her body may still be constipated. That bloating and fullness she was feeling— along with the cramping—can often be caused by stool that is sitting in the bowel and not moving properly.

Sophie was shocked—no one had ever explained this to her before. But when she thought about it, it made sense. The constant bloating, the feeling of never fully emptying, and the cycles of loose stool and cramping all added up.

I advised Sophie that in cases like this, supporting the gut with soothing products like REZCUE can be helpful, but the first step must be to gently address the underlying constipation. Products like Move and Daily Healthy Fibre could be great starting points to help retrain the bowel and get things moving properly.

We also emphasised the importance of going slow and gentle, as clearing out a backed-up bowel takes time—and sudden changes could make her symptoms worse if not done carefully.

For Sophie, this was a turning point. After years of focusing on "fixing diarrhea," she now understood her body in a completely new way—and finally had a path forward. It took almost a week of taking Move, building the dosage slowly, but eventually Sophie started having proper movements for the first time in years. We introduced Daily Healthy Fibre into her diet, which is now part of her daily routine.

> *"I thought I had IBS for years, but turns out it was hidden constipation, I would never have thought this could be a thing. Daily Healthy Fibre and Move made everything regular again, and the bloating just stopped. I can't imagine life without THERA Nordic."*
>
> *- Sophie*

Lisa's Story: The Overwhelming Struggle with SIBO and Candida

Symptoms: Bloating, Brain fog, Fatigue, SIBO, Candida

Lisa, a 42-year-old and mother of one, had been dealing with debilitating digestive issues for years. What began as occasional bloating and tiredness had gradually spiraled into daily struggles with her gut—and her life.

She described severe bloating that made her look "six months pregnant" by the end of the day, constant brain fog, fatigue, and a frustrating cycle of loose stools alternating with constipation. But what made things even worse were the sugar cravings she couldn't control and the frequent yeast infections that kept coming back no matter what she did.

Lisa had tried every diet under the sun—low FODMAP, gluten-free, dairy-free. She had experimented with probiotics, antifungals, herbal remedies, but nothing seemed to give her long-term relief. She felt like she was constantly fighting a battle on two fronts—one against SIBO (Small Intestinal Bacterial Overgrowth) and another against Candida overgrowth.

How we helped

Feeling overwhelmed, she reached out us, sharing her long history of symptoms and asking if there was anything that could help her "reset" her gut.

After reading her story carefully, I acknowledged how exhausting and frustrating her journey had been. I explained that SIBO and Candida often go hand-in-hand, especially when the gut is compromised, and the immune system is overwhelmed. Both conditions can feed each other—with Candida exploiting the weakened gut barrier caused by SIBO, and SIBO worsening due to the toxic byproducts of yeast overgrowth.

But most importantly, we shared two key messages:

1. Healing is possible—but it requires a structured, step-by-step approach, and trying to tackle everything at once can often make things worse.
2. Because of the complex nature of SIBO and Candida together, it's vital to work with a healthcare professional—someone who can guide her through the right testing (like SIBO breath tests and Candida markers), track her progress, and adjust treatment as her body responds.

I recommended that once she had a professional to oversee her healing, starting with gut-calming and barrier-repairing products like REZCUE could be a gentle first step—helping reduce gut inflammation and begin restoring the mucosal lining.

Then, in time, targeted anti-microbial support like Bacti-Balance could be introduced to help rebalance gut flora, combined with Daily Healthy Fibre to nourish beneficial bacteria. But timing would be crucial to avoid die-off reactions that could make her symptoms worse.

I also advised that trying to tackle SIBO or Candida alone, especially when both are present, can be overwhelming and sometimes make symptoms worse. But we assured her that we would be there to support her on the journey.

Lisa was grateful for the honesty and care in the response. For the first time, she didn't feel pushed into a quick fix. Instead, she had a clear understanding of what was happening in her body—and a realistic plan to begin healing with the right support.

Her story reminds us that gut healing is a journey, not a race, and compassionate, informed guidance makes all the difference.

My gut felt out of control—bloating, sugar cravings, brain fog, the lot. Following THERA Nordic's plan gave me structure, and for once, things started to actually work. The customer service far outweighed any support I've ever had from a doctor."

- Lisa

Tom's Story: Living with Daily Diarrhea and No Answers

Tom, a 36-year-old teacher, had been living with daily diarrhea for over two years. What started as an occasional upset stomach had turned into a constant struggle, impacting his work, social life, and overall confidence.

Every morning, Tom had to plan his day around toilet access. He often avoided eating breakfast, knowing that any food could send him rushing to the bathroom within minutes. Even simple meals didn't seem safe anymore. After every meal, his stomach would cramp, gurgle, and churn, and the urgent need to go would soon follow.

Tom had seen multiple doctors. He was tested for parasites, infections, and celiac disease—all came back negative. His GP told him it might be IBS-D (irritable bowel syndrome with Diarrhea) and recommended cutting out gluten and dairy, but even after months of restrictive eating, nothing had really changed.

How we helped

Frustrated and at a loss for what to do next, Tom came to us, asking if anything natural could help calm his digestion and give him his life back.

When I read Tom's story, I could see the exhaustion in his words. I started by acknowledging that chronic diarrhea is incredibly draining—both physically and emotionally—and that he wasn't alone in facing this challenge.

But I also explained an important point that many people don't realise; Diarrhea can sometimes be a sign of a deeper gut issue, like inflammation, a compromised gut lining, or even 'hidden' constipation. To address it properly, it is essential to look at the root cause.

I advised Tom that while soothing and healing the gut lining with something like REZCUE could be a great first step to reduce irritation and calm the digestive tract, it would be vital for him to explore underlying causes such as:

- SIBO (Small Intestinal Bacterial Overgrowth)
- Bile acid malabsorption
- Inflammatory bowel disease (IBD)

I explained that if his diarrhea had been going on this long, a stool analysis and possibly a SIBO test could be very helpful in understanding what's happening in his gut.

At the same time, I suggested that adding digestive support like Optimized Enzymes could be considered to help improve food breakdown and reduce irritation along with Daily Healthy Fibre. Fibre can seem a scary word for someone suffering with diarrhea, but it can be very helpful in the healing process. Adding a gentle fibre like Daily Healthy Fibre will help add bulk to the stools, balance gut bacteria, slow the movement of food through the digestive tract allowing more nutrients to be absorbed. Fibre will also help with inflammation and irritation in the digestive tract. It took a bit of convincing to get Tom to try the fibre, but he very quickly started noticeable changes.

I also reassured Tom that he did not have to live like this, and he should not feel like he was out of options. With the right support and testing, many people do get answers and start feeling better.

"I had constant diarrhea for two years, and nothing helped. Starting slow with REZCUE made a big difference—it's the first time I've felt like things are returning to normal."

- Tom

💡 Quick Tip: Hydrate, Hydrate, Hydrate

Drink **enough water throughout the day** to keep the digestive system moving and prevent constipation.

Sip water **between meals** rather than during meals to avoid diluting stomach acid.

Closing Chapter: Your Gut Healing Journey Starts Here

If you've made it this far, I want to say thank you. Thank you for investing in yourself, for being open to learning, and for taking the time to understand what true health really looks like.

Gut health is at the core of so much — not just digestion, but our energy, mood, immune system, hormones, and so much more. And yet, for many of us, this vital part of our health has been overlooked, misunderstood, or even dismissed.

I hope that by reading this book, you've realised a few important things:

You are not broken.

If you've been struggling with gut issues, know that there *is* a way forward. You don't need to live on restrictive diets, endless supplements, or in constant fear of food. Your body wants to heal — and with the right support, it can.

It's never just one thing.

Gut health is not only about what you eat or what supplements you take. It's about how you live, how you move, how you sleep, how you manage stress, and how connected you feel to others. The six core pillars of health work together to support each other. Healing happens when we address the whole picture.

Small steps lead to big changes.

You don't have to be perfect. You don't have to overhaul your entire life overnight. Healing your gut and transforming your health is about progress, not perfection. Small, consistent choices — like eating more fibre, walking after meals, or getting to bed earlier — add up over time.

You deserve to feel good in your body.

You deserve to wake up feeling energised, to enjoy food without fear, to live without bloating, pain, or fatigue. And it's possible — no matter how long you've been struggling.

Where to Go from Here

If you're wondering what the "next step" is — here's what I recommend:

1. Start with the basics. Go back to the six pillars and choose just one or two small changes to begin your journey. Maybe it's focusing on chewing your food properly, adding one new vegetable to your meals, or taking a short walk after dinner. Don't try and change too much too quickly.

2. Be gentle with yourself. Healing is not a straight line. You'll have good days and not-so-good days. That's normal. Be patient and compassionate — you're doing something amazing for yourself.

3. Listen to your body. No expert knows your body better than you do. If something feels good, keep doing it. If something feels off, pause and reassess. Your body is always sending you messages. Not all advice on social media is bad. But be wary of quick fixes or generic advice. You are now armed with more knowledge to approach advice with healthy skepticism and work out if it's something that is right for your body.

4. Reach out for support if you need it. Whether that's working with a practitioner, connecting with others on a similar journey, or even sending us a message at THERA Nordic — don't do this alone. Community makes a world of difference.

A Personal Note from Me

If you take just one thing away from this book, let it be this: Your gut can heal, and you are worthy of that healing.

I've been where you are. I know what it feels like to try everything and still not feel better. But I also know the freedom that comes when things start to shift — when digestion works the way it's meant to, when energy returns, and when life stops revolving around symptoms.

That's why THERA Nordic exists. Not to sell you a cupboard full of supplements, but to remind you that healing is possible, and to offer real, effective tools backed by science — tools that can support you on this journey, not define it.

And finally…

Thank you for trusting me to walk this part of your health journey with you. I hope this book has given you some insight, hope, and a starting point for real change.

So now, it's over to you — Start small. Stay curious. Trust your body. And above all, keep going.

Because you've got this. And we're right here, cheering you on.

With love and belief in you,

Emma xx

Appendix I: References & Further Reading

Here are a selection of books, articles and papers that have been inspirational to me. Professor Tim Spector and Dr Will Bulsiewicz I've mentioned in the book, but they have published some particularly great work. I've included the QR codes which you can scan with your phone to easily find the links if you're interested in reading any of these.

Outlive: The Science and Art of Longevity

Peter Attia MD

Peter Attiia is one of my favourite doctors. I highly recommend listening to his podcast or following him on Instagram.

Fibre Fueled

By Dr Will Bulsiewicz.

My "go-to" book on fibre, but also a great scientific overview of the latest studies on the microbiome that debunk many of the fad diets that have focused on eliminating specific food groups.

The Food for Life Cookbook

By Professor Tim Spector

An amazing cookbook from the founder of the ZOE project and someone who is really leading the way in the latest gut health science.

Spoon-Fed: Why almost everything we've been told about food is wrong

By Professor Tim Spector

As the title implies, this is a great book which debunks a lot of the traditional myths that we've grown up with about what we eat. I can't recommend this one highly enough!

The Little Book on Enzymes

By Joni Laiho

This free eBook is available on the THERA Nordic website and provides a brief but incredibly comprehensive overview of the role of enzymes in the gut.

The THERA Nordic Health Blog

By Emma Cannings & Joni Laiho

You'll find articles on here about most of the topics covered in this book as well as information about the science behind our products.

Fiber and Prebiotics: Mechanisms and Health Benefits

By Joanne Slavin

For those of you who want to get further into the science, this is a really interesting paper which covers a lot of the benefits of fibre in gut health and the links to improved cardiovascular health.

Uncovering the Mysteries of the Gut–Brain Connection

By Helen Albert

"Inside Precision Medicine" is a fantastic online publication and this article does a great job of delving further into the gut-brain connection.

Gut

By Guilia Enders

This is a Sunday Times bestseller from an author featured on Netflix's Hack Your Health: the secrets of your gut. This book also dives into the connection with mental health with its focus on the gut-brain link.

Hack Your Health

Netflix

I am often cautious about recommending documentaries as they can sometimes present relatively biased views on a specific approach. However, for those of you who have Netflix, this has been mostly praised by the professional community for giving a valuable introduction into the importance of good gut health.

Appendix II: Recipes

Gut-Healing High-Fibre Morning Smoothie: **My everyday breakfast**

Ingredients (Serves 1):

- **1/2 avocado** (creamy texture, healthy fats, and fibre)
- **1 tbsp chia seeds OR ground flaxseeds** (prebiotic fibre + omega-3)
- **1/2 cooked/steamed then frozen courgette** (gentle fibre and natural sweetness — courgette option for low sugar)
- **1 scoop clean protein powder** (collagen, whey, or plant-based — optional but great for balancing blood sugar)
- **1 tsp cinnamon** (helps balance blood sugar and supports digestion)
- **250-300ml unsweetened almond milk or coconut water** (or any milk of choice)
- 1/4 cup frozen berries (blueberries/raspberries for polyphenols and extra fibre)
- 1 x Scoop of Daily Healthy Fibre
- Sprinkle of seeds once blended

Avocado & Seeded Toast:
Savory, High Fibre

Ingredients:

- 1 slice whole grain or seeded bread (look for 4g+ fibre per slice)
- ½ ripe avocado (fibre + healthy fats)
- 1 tsp chia seeds or hemp seeds (for extra fibre & omega-3)
- A squeeze of lemon juice
- Salt & pepper to taste
- Optional: sliced tomatoes, radish, or cucumber on top

Method:

1. Toast the bread to your liking.
2. Mash avocado with lemon juice, salt, and pepper.
3. Spread on toast and sprinkle with seeds.
4. Add veggies if desired for extra fibre and freshness.

Fibre boost: ~8–10g fibre depending on bread & toppings

Greek Yogurt & Apple Fibre Bowl:
Protein + Fibre

Ingredients:

- ¾ cup Greek yogurt (plain, unsweetened)
- 1 small apple, chopped with skin on (fibre-rich)
- 1 tbsp ground flaxseed or psyllium husk (huge fibre boost)
- 1 tbsp chopped nuts (almonds or walnuts)
- Dash of cinnamon
- Optional: drizzle of honey or a few raisins

Method:

1. Mix yogurt, chopped apple, flaxseed, and cinnamon.
2. Top with nuts and drizzle honey if desired.
3. Enjoy as a quick, protein and fibre-packed breakfast.

Fibre boost: ~8–10g fibre

Bonus Tip #1: Pair these with a **glass of water or herbal tea** to help fibre work smoothly in your system and support post-surgery healing.

Bonus Tip #2: Boosting Fibre in Lunches:

- **Add seeds** (flax, chia, pumpkin) to salads and bowls.
- Choose **whole grains** (brown rice, quinoa, bulgur, barley).
- Add a **small side of beans, lentils, or roasted chickpeas** to any dish.
- Pair with a side of **fruit** (apple, pear, berries) for extra fibre.

Warm Sweet Potato & Black Bean Bowl:
Fibre-rich lunch with plant proteins and complex carbs

Ingredients (Serves 2):

- 1 large sweet potato, cubed (I always batch cook my sweet potatoes so they are at hand for a quick lunch)
- 1 can (400g) black beans, drained and rinsed
- 1/2 red pepper, diced
- 1/2 avocado, sliced
- 1/4 cup fresh coriander, chopped
- 1 tbsp olive oil or avocado oil
- 1/2 tsp smoked paprika
- 1/2 tsp cumin
- Salt & pepper to taste
- Lime wedges to serve

Instructions:

1. Preheat oven to 200°C (400°F). Toss sweet potato cubes with olive oil, paprika, cumin, salt, and pepper. Spread on a baking tray and roast for 20-25 minutes until soft and slightly crisp.

2. While the sweet potato is roasting, warm the black beans in a small pan over low heat.
3. To serve, divide sweet potatoes and black beans between bowls. Top with red pepper, avocado slices, and chopped coriander.
4. Squeeze over fresh lime juice before serving.

Fibre boost: Black beans, sweet potato, veggies — **14-16g fibre per bowl**.

Mediterranean Chickpea & Quinoa Salad:
Packed with fibre, plant-based protein, and healthy fats.

Ingredients (Serves 2-3):

- 1 cup cooked quinoa (cooled)
- 1 can (400g) chickpeas, drained and rinsed
- 1 cup cherry tomatoes, halved
- 1/2 cucumber, diced
- 1/4 red onion, finely chopped
- 1/4 cup olives, sliced
- 1/4 cup feta cheese (optional)
- 1/4 cup fresh parsley or mint, chopped
- **For dressing:**
    - 3 tbsp extra virgin olive oil
    - Juice of 1 lemon
    - 1 tsp Dijon mustard
    - 1 garlic clove, minced
    - Salt & pepper to taste

Instructions:

1. In a large bowl, combine quinoa, chickpeas, tomatoes, cucumber, red onion, olives, feta, and herbs.
2. In a small bowl, whisk together the olive oil, lemon juice, mustard, garlic, salt, and pepper.
3. Pour dressing over the salad and toss well to combine.
4. Serve immediately or store in the fridge for a chilled option.

Fibre boost: Chickpeas, quinoa, veggies — around **10-12g fibre per serving**.

Grilled Chicken & Fibre-Packed Power Bowl:

A nourishing, high-fibre lunch with lean animal protein, colourful veggies, and healthy fats.

Ingredients (Serves 2):

For the Bowl:

- 2 free-range chicken breasts (organic if possible)
- 1 cup cooked brown rice or quinoa (fibre-rich base)
- 1 cup steamed broccoli florets
- 1/2 cup roasted or steamed carrots (sliced)
- 1/2 cup shredded red cabbage (raw for crunch & fibre)
- 1/4 avocado, sliced
- 2 tbsp pumpkin seeds (optional, for crunch and extra fibre)
- 1 tbsp olive oil (for cooking)

For the Dressing:

- 2 tbsp extra virgin olive oil
- 1 tbsp apple cider vinegar or lemon juice (great for digestion)
- 1 tsp Dijon mustard
- 1 tsp honey or maple syrup (optional, for sweetness)
- Salt & pepper to taste

Instructions:

1. **Prepare the Chicken:**
   - Season chicken breasts with salt, pepper, and a sprinkle of smoked paprika or herbs of choice.
   - Heat olive oil in a pan over medium heat. Cook chicken breasts for 6–7 minutes on each side until fully cooked and juices run clear. Let rest for 5 minutes, then slice.
2. **Prepare the Veggies & Grains:**
   - While the chicken cooks, steam broccoli and carrots until tender but still vibrant.
   - Shred red cabbage and slice avocado.
   - Prepare rice or quinoa as per packet instructions if not already done.
3. **Make the Dressing:**
   - Whisk all dressing ingredients together in a small bowl. Adjust seasoning to taste.
4. **Assemble the Bowl:**
   - In each bowl, layer rice/quinoa, steamed veggies, cabbage, and sliced chicken.
   - Top with avocado and pumpkin seeds.
   - Drizzle over the dressing and enjoy!

One-Pan Mediterranean Chicken & Vegetable Bake:

High Fibre + High Protein

Ingredients (Serves 2-3):

- 2 free-range chicken thighs or breasts (skin on for added healthy fats, optional)
- 1 medium red onion, chopped
- 1 large courgette, chopped
- 1 red bell pepper, chopped
- 1 cup cherry tomatoes, halved
- 1/2 cup cooked chickpeas (or butter beans for extra fibre and creaminess)
- 3 garlic cloves, minced
- 2 tbsp extra virgin olive oil
- 1 tsp dried oregano
- 1 tsp smoked paprika
- Salt & pepper to taste
- Juice of 1/2 lemon
- Fresh parsley to garnish

Instructions:

1. **Preheat oven** to 200°C (400°F).
2. Toss all chopped vegetables, chickpeas, and garlic with olive oil, oregano, paprika, salt, and pepper in a baking tray.
3. Nestle the chicken thighs/breasts among the vegetables. Drizzle lemon juice over everything.
4. **Bake** for 30–35 minutes, turning veggies halfway through, until chicken is fully cooked and veggies are tender.
5. Garnish with fresh parsley and serve.

Fibre boost:

- Chickpeas, courgette, peppers, and tomatoes add **soluble and insoluble fibre**.
- Hearty, filling, and great for batch cooking!

Lentil & Beef Shepherd's Pie:
Protein & Fibre Packed Comfort Food

Ingredients (Serves 4):

- 300g grass-fed minced beef (or lamb)
- 1 cup cooked green or brown lentils (adds fibre and reduces total meat load)
- 1 onion, diced
- 2 garlic cloves, minced
- 1 carrot, diced
- 1 celery stalk, diced
- 1 cup frozen peas
- 1 tbsp tomato paste
- 1 tsp dried thyme
- 1 tsp smoked paprika (optional)
- 2 tbsp olive oil or butter
- Salt & pepper to taste

For the mash topping:

- 2 large sweet potatoes or regular potatoes (or mix)
- 1 tbsp olive oil or butter
- Splash of milk (dairy or non-dairy)
- Salt & pepper

Instructions:

1. **Boil potatoes** until soft, mash with olive oil/butter and milk. Set aside.
2. **Sauté** onion, garlic, carrot, and celery in oil until soft.
3. Add minced beef and brown well. Stir in lentils, tomato paste, thyme, paprika, and seasonings. Add a splash of water if needed to loosen. Stir in peas.
4. Transfer beef/lentil mix to a baking dish. Top with mashed potatoes.
5. **Bake** at 180°C (350°F) for 20–25 mins until golden.

Fibre boost:

- Lentils, peas, carrots, and potatoes add **a diverse fibre profile**.
- A perfect blend of comfort and gut health!

Salmon & Roasted Veg Traybake with Quinoa & Lemon Dressing:

Anti-inflammatory + High Fibre

Ingredients (Serves 2-3):

- 2 salmon fillets (wild-caught if possible)
- 1 cup cooked quinoa (high fibre and high protein)
- 1 cup broccoli florets
- 1/2 head cauliflower, cut into florets
- 1/2 cup asparagus (or green beans)
- 1 red onion, sliced
- 2 tbsp olive oil
- Salt, pepper, and turmeric or cumin for seasoning

Lemon Dressing:

- Juice of 1 lemon
- 2 tbsp extra virgin olive oil
- 1 tsp Dijon mustard
- 1 tsp honey (optional)
- Salt & pepper

Instructions:

1. **Preheat oven** to 200°C (400°F).
2. Toss broccoli, cauliflower, asparagus, and red onion with olive oil and spices on a tray. Roast for 20 minutes.
3. Add salmon fillets to the tray, season, and roast another 10–12 minutes until cooked.
4. Meanwhile, cook quinoa and whisk together dressing ingredients.
5. Serve roasted veg and salmon over quinoa, drizzled with dressing.

Fibre boost:

- Quinoa, broccoli, cauliflower, asparagus = **gut-loving fibre**.
- Omega-3s from salmon for anti-inflammatory benefits!

Apple Slices with Almond Butter:
Simple, Crunchy, Satisfying

Ingredients:

- 1 apple, sliced
- 1 tbsp almond butter (or other nut butter)

Greek Yogurt (or Coconut Yogurt):
Creamy + Probiotic + Fibre

Ingredients:

- 150g full-fat Greek yogurt or unsweetened coconut yogurt (for dairy-free)
- 1 tbsp ground flaxseed or chia seeds or Daily Healthy Fibre
- Handful of berries or pomegranate seeds
- Optional: sprinkle of pumpkin seeds for crunch

Trail Mix (Homemade, No Added Sugar):
Portable, Fibre-Packed Energy Boost

Ingredients:

- Handful of mixed nuts (almonds, walnuts, pecans)
- Pumpkin seeds or sunflower seeds
- A sprinkle of unsweetened coconut flakes

Cottage Cheese or Yogurt Bowl with Seeds & Cinnamon:
Protein + Fibre + Probiotic

Ingredients:

- 150g cottage cheese (or Greek yogurt/coconut yogurt)
- 1 tbsp ground flaxseed or chia seeds or Daily Healthy Fibre
- Sprinkle of sunflower or pumpkin seeds
- Dash of cinnamon, optional berries

Stuffed Medjool Dates with Nut Butter:
Sweet, Satisfying, Fibre-Rich

Ingredients:

- 2-3 Medjool dates
- Filled with almond or peanut butter

Appendix III: Using THERA Nordic Products

At THERA Nordic, our goal is not to create products you'll need to take for life. Instead, we want to support your body as it heals and rebalances, so you can eventually move on without being dependent on supplements — but with support available whenever you need it.

Most of our products are designed to help you through a healing or rebuilding phase, where your gut needs extra support. Once healing has taken place, you may no longer need them daily—you might just use them during flare-ups or challenging periods.

Below is a breakdown of each product, how and why to use it along with information on some of the more common combinations of the products. The QR code next to each product will take you through to our "The Science Behind" articles, which explains the science behind the product formulation with links to relevant scientific sources. Now that you have a more solid grounding in gut health, hopefully you'll get a lot more from those articles.

REZCUE

REZCUE treats leaky gut and prevents acid reflux and heartburn by soothing and repairing the gut lining via the dual effects from our unique combination of Zinc Carnosine and L-Glutamine, both scientifically proven to be highly beneficial for the GI tract.

In addition, zinc is vital for many important functions of the body including a strong immune system good skin health. And Carnosine is one of the most important anti-aging nutrients.

As the powder is consumed in a 100% water-soluble drink it immediately soothes the mucosal lining from the mouth to the stomach and the small and large intestines.

Key Benefits

- Renews & protects the gut
- Treats leaky gut
- Fast relief for acid reflux
- No fillers or preservatives
- Scientifically proven ingredients

Ingredients

L-Glutamine, Zinc Carnosine (L-Carnosine + Zinc Acetate complex)

Amounts per serving (1 scoop / 2500mg):

- Zinc: **8 mg**
- L-Carnosine: **29.5 mg**
- L-Glutamine: **2438 mg**

How to Use

Mix one scoop (2.5g) of powder in warm (not boiling!) liquid and take twice daily, in the morning and in the evening. The dose in the evening is best taken before bed.

REZCUE works best taken in empty stomach, but if you feel any discomfort, you can take it with small amount of food as well.

Note on thyroid medications. Please have at least 1 hour between REZCUE and taking your medication as these may inhibit each other's efficiency.

The Science Behind REZCUE

Scan the QR code learn more about **why Zinc Carnosine is far more effective when combined with L-Glutamine** and how this powder targets inflammation.

Triple HCL

Triple HCL supports healthy digestion in three ways.

1. Betaine HCL increases the amount of hydrochloric acid in the stomach, crucial for digesting proteins, killing harmful bacteria, and absorbing minerals and vitamins from our food. Stress and ageing in particular can cause reduction in stomach acid.
2. Natural bitters stimulate the natural hydrochloric acid and bile acid secretion for complete digestion of food
3. Pepsin, a protein-digesting enzyme, helps in the digestion of both proteins in the food, as well as digesting away the harmful bacteria.

These improvements help to resolve the underlying issues that can cause heartburn, acid reflux, indigestion, bloating, general discomfort, post-meal fatigue and minimise the risk of constipation.

Please note that this product is not suitable for vegans or vegetarians.

Key Benefits

- Restores a healthy pH level in the stomach
- Fast relief from bloating, indigestion and discomfort
- Can prevent heartburn, acid reflux & constipation
- Improves absorption of nutrients & protein digestion
- Kills harmful bacteria

Ingredients

Betaine hydrochloride, Yellow gentian (Gentiana Lutea) root extract, Pepsin (porcine), HPMC (Capsule)

Amounts per serving (1 capsule)

- Betaine Hydrochloride: **500 mg**
- Gentiana lutea extract: **50 mg**
- Pepsin enzyme: **25,000 NF**

How to Use

- Start with 1 capsule with each meal.
- If your symptoms don't change after 2 days, increase to 2 capsules per meal.

- Repeat this process as needed and work up to 4 capsules per meal.
- Stay with the dose that feels best, no need to take more.
- If you feel any discomfort, irritation, or other side effects, reduce the dose.

Only take with meals, never on empty stomach.

The Science Behind Triple HCL

Scan the QR code to **learn more about how this betaine HCL supplement can support low stomach acid production,** a condition known as "hypochlorhydria".

Optimized Enzymes

Optimized Enzymes is an advanced enzyme formula to enhance the digestion of food. It helps digest the whole meal and eliminate gas, bloating and other symptoms of indigestion.

By improving the digestion of proteins, taking a digestive enzyme also helps to enhance muscle mass.

Optimized Enzymes contains a special enzyme, which specifically targets the proteins that can cause sensitivity to the gluten in wheat. This special enzyme also digests milk proteins.

Key Benefits

- Relief from bloating, indigestion and discomfort
- Effectively digests gluten & milk proteins
- Improves absorption of nutrients & enhances digestion
- Cleanses and detoxes when taken on an empty stomach before bed

Ingredients

Protease, Amylase, Alpha-galactosidase, Cellulase, DPP-IV, Glucoamylase, Invertase, Lactase, Lipase, Phytase, Xylanase, Hypromellose (capsule)

Amounts per serving (1 capsule):

- Acid Stable Protease: **100 SAPU**
- Protease: **90,000 HUT**
- Amylase: **25,000 DU**
- Alpha-galactosidase: **800 GALU**
- Cellulase: **1,500 CU**
- Gluten & Casein targeting enzyme: **1050 DPPU**
- Glucoamylase: **55 AGU**
- Invertase: **400 SU**
- Lactase: **1,000 ALU**
- Lipase: **3,500 FIP**
- Phytase: **45 FTU**
- Xylanase: **725 XU**

How to Use

Take one capsule three times a day with a meal.

Two capsules can also be taken on an empty stomach before bed for additional benefits.

Do not use if you have an active gastric ulcer.

The Science Behind Optimized Enzymes

Scan the QR code to learn more about the science behind **how this digestive enzyme supports your digestion.**

Move

Move is a natural and gentle way to effectively detox the gut and stimulate healthy bowel movements. Move first softens the bowel contents and then stimulates natural movement through a combination of magnesium and kiwi.

Key Benefits

- Relief from constipation
- Promotes healthy bowel mobility
- Soothes the gut lining
- Gentle action

Ingredients

Magnesium Hydroxide, magnesium citrate, kiwi fruit extract (Actazin)

Amounts per serving (1 capsule):

- Magnesium: **85 mg** (as magnesium hydroxide & citrate)
- Kiwi fruit extract (Actazin): **300 mg**

How to Use

- Take 2 capsules before bed.
- If there is a bowel movement next day, this is your dose.
- If not, increase to 4 capsules on the next night. You can go up to six capsules. Adjust to the dose that is exactly right for you.

The Science Behind Move

Scan the QR code to learn more about the **3 core, science-backed reasons why Move is superior** to many of the standard laxatives on the market today.

Daily Healthy Fibre

Daily Healthy Fibre is a great source of fibre which provides a wide range of health benefits from improved regulation of blood sugar to better heart health.

Fibre can help you feel fuller for longer so can be a great help for those looking for support with their weight management.

Daily Healthy Fibre is a high-quality prebiotic fibre, feeding your body's probiotics in order to improve the composition of your gut microbiome, improving your overall gut health and enhancing the absorption of nutrients.

Key Benefits

- Helps to ensure regular bowel movements
- Acts as a prebiotic to improve your overall digestive health
- Keeps you full for longer to help with weight management
- Fibre can regulate blood sugar levels
- IBS & FODMAP friendly

Ingredients

Inavea (Acacia fiber, Baobab powder), Sunfiber (partially hydrolyzed agar gum)

Amounts per serving (1 scoop / 8000 mg):

- **Inavea ™** (Acacia + Baobab): **5000 mg**
- **Sunfiber ™** (hydrolyzed guar gum): **3000 mg**

How to Use

- Just mix one scoop into smoothies, juice, yogurt, porridge, drinks or food.
- Take up to 3 scoops per day.

The Science Behind Daily Healthy Fibre

Scan the QR code to learn more about **the three soluble fibre superstars that we used for Daily Healthy Fibre:** guar beans, baobab fruit and acacia.

Bacti-Balance

Bacti-Balance is a natural antioxidant, boosting immunity, cleansing the intestine and balancing the gut microbiome through the powerful combination of high potent garlic extract and oregano oil.

The delivery of the ingredients is highly targeted to the small intestine via our specialised enteric coated capsules.

Bacti-Balance is not just for those that suffer with SIBO or SIFO. It can be highly effective for anyone suffering from the common symptoms of these issues, including:

- Bloating and Gas
- Abdominal pain or discomfort
- Food intolerances
- Chronic fatigue

Key Benefits

- Treats SIBO, SIFO and Candida
- Delayed release capsule for targeted action
- Eliminates unfriendly bacteria
- Balances the gut microbiome

Ingredients

Garlic Extract, Modified Tapioca Starch, (Delayed release capsule: HPMC, Gellan gum), Oregano Oil powder, Potato Maltodextrin, Rice Fibre

Amounts per serving (1 capsule):

- Allicin **5000 mcg**
- Carvarcol (from Oregano): **36 mg**

How to Use

Bacti-Balance is a natural antibiotic and like pharmaceutical antibiotics it is best taken as a course.

1 capsule, 3 times per day with a meal. A course of 40-60 days (2-3 bottles) is recommended.

⚛ The Science Behind Bacti-Balance

Scan the QR code to **learn more about the research into the benefits of oregano oil and garlic.**

Common Combinations of our products

Here are some of the most common combinations of our products that can be used to target more challenging gut health issues. These are based on the treatment plans that we have developed at THERA Nordic. In each case you'll find a QR code that you can scan if you would like more details on the plans, including exactly how the products should be taken.

Heartburn and Indigestion

Products: REZCUE, Daily Healthy Fibre, Optimized Enzymes and Triple HCL

There is always a degree of inflammation associated with heartburn, so the first step is to start with REZCUE. Soothing the inflammation and irritation in the stomach and intestine enables proper digestion. Incomplete and slow digestion is one cause for acid reflux.

After a week or so the Optimized Enzymes are added to help digest and absorb the food. This accelerates the digestion and helps with digestion of nutrients. Daily Healthy Fibre can also be added to your meals so that we are introducing a prebiotic fibre to support the good bacteria in the gut.

Finally, after calming and supporting the stomach, we will start strengthening the production of stomach acid with Triple HCL.

For me personally, it was the Triple HCL which was the game changer! For others, their body just needs some enzyme support with Optimized Enzymes. But you can now hopefully see how these different products would come together to help solve some of the underlying issues that might be causing the heartburn and indigestion.

Heartburn & Indigestion: 28-day plan

Scan the QR code for details on THERA Nordic's **Heartburn & Indigestion 28-day plan.**

IBS & Bloating

Products: REZCUE, Daily Healthy Fibre, Optimized Enzymes and Triple HCL

Irritable Bowel Syndrome is an imbalance of the gut. Alongside the use of supplements we always recommend that people follow a FODMAP diet for which there are many plans that you can find online that will take you through the steps of identifying the foods that might be causing you the most issues.

Again, initially we encourage people to start on REZCUE for at least a week in order to heal any underlying inflammation that has been caused and calming the intestinal lining. Then we bring in Optimized Enzymes, which will often help to further ease the irritation. Next, we use Triple HCL to start strengthening the stomach acids to healthy levels, to make sure no more bad bacteria have access to the bowel, and to facilitate complete digestion.

The final step is to start using Daily Healthy Fibre in order to introduce a gentle prebiotic to feed the good bacteria in the gut.

🗓 IBS & Bloating: 28-day plan

Scan the QR code for details on THERA Nordic's **IBS & Bloating 28-day plan.**

Chronic Constipation

Products: Move, Daily Healthy Fibre, Optimized Enzymes and Triple HCL

For anyone with constipation (chronic or otherwise), we would always start them off with Move in order to clear and detoxify the bowel. Building on this foundation we then add Daily Healthy Fibre to nourish the gut microbiome and support natural regularity.

The final step is to give the digestion itself a boost by strengthening the stomach acids and enzymatic activity. Again, for some it's the Triple HCL which helps the most, for others it's Optimized Enzymes, or a combination of both. Since it's not easy to test for low stomach acid it tends to be a bit of a trial-and-error approach. But don't worry, the body is very clever with betaine HCL supplements like Triple HCL and won't increase your HCL beyond optimum levels for your body.

Chronic Constipation: 28-day plan

Scan the QR code for details on THERA Nordic's **Chronic Constipation 28-day plan.**

SIBO and Candida

Products: Bacti-Balance, REZCUE, Optimized Enzymes or Triple HCL

SIBO (Small Intestine Bacterial Overgrowth) and Candida overgrowth are recognised imbalances that can cause similar digestive symptoms. However, they require a targeted approach to address their root causes effectively.

Bacti-Balance is the key product here, and many people experience great results with it alone. However, combining it with other products can provide even better outcomes for both bacterial and fungal imbalances.

We combine Bacti-Balance alongside Triple HCL (or Optimized Enzymes for vegans/vegetarians) and REZCUE for an initial 6-week period.

This combination is particularly effective because addressing both bacterial and fungal overgrowth while supporting digestion and gut lining repair provides a more comprehensive approach to tackling both SIBO and Candida overgrowth effectively.

SIBO & Candida: 6-week plan

Scan the QR code for details on THERA Nordic's **SIBO & Candida 6-week plan.**